ALCHEMY

ANIMA MERCVRII

JAY RAMSAY

ALCHEMY

THE ART OF TRANSFORMATION

WITH ILLUSTRATIONS BY HELEN ELWES

Thorsons
An Imprint of HarperCollinsPublishers

Thorsons
An Imprint of HarperCollins*Publishers*
77–85 Fulham Palace Road
Hammersmith, London W6 8JB
1160 Battery Street
San Francisco, California 94111–1213

Published by Thorsons 1997

10 9 8 7 6 5 4 3 2

A catalogue record for this book
is available from the British Library

ISBN 1 85538 509 0

Illustrations by Helen Elwes, drawn fron sixteenth
and seventeenth century woodcuts

Printed and bound in Great Britain by
Creative Print and Design (Wales), Ebbw Vale

Pray, read, re-read and work – and you will find.

MUTUS LIBER

for you

Study me then, you who shall lovers bee,
At the next world, that is at the next Spring,
For I am every dead thing
In whom love wrought new Alchimie.

JOHN DONNE, 'A NOCTURNALL UPON ST LUCIE'S DAY'

CONTENTS

FOREWORD

Jay Ramsay has written a luminous and wise guide to the mysteries of soul and to the images and texts of alchemy which explore these mysteries, extending an invitation to us to 'visit the interior of the earth' – that unknown territory that is both within and around us. Alchemy is the key, lost for centuries, that gives us the way to reconnect with the soul, to come to know and understand it and to release it from the prison of our neglect of it. Alchemy is, as he says, the missing aspect of our own religious tradition that we look for beyond our own culture, the missing key to the understanding of our nature and to the transformation of that nature from base metal into gold. Belief has never been enough to transform the suffering of humanity nor to bring to an end the endless repetition of human barbarism. Alchemy is a science which teaches the way to the transformation and to that inner marriage which gives us deep insight into life and to the complexes which stand in the way of a creative relationship with the soul. No one can write about alchemy who is not living it and no one can pass on his or her knowledge and insight who has not walked the difficult path of self-discovery. A guide is not someone who has arrived, but someone who accompanies us as we search for the treasure and who has experienced something of the 'darkness darker than darkness' and the meaning of the 'wondrous stone'.

ANNE BARING

ACKNOWLEDGEMENTS

In every sense this book is the harvest of a group effort, although one hand actually wrote it; but this one hand couldn't have moved as it did without all I've been given over the seven years of experience and study that formed the basis and *prima materia* of it. So I want royally to thank the following as co-facilitators in all their various ways:

Alison Roberts (author of *Hathor Rising*), who first saw alchemy in me; Carole Bruce, who above all nurtured its seed; Barbara Somers, who gave it so freely through her lecture notes; Bronwen Astor, who gave me invaluable house room to 'fall through'; Glenn Storhaug (of Five Seasons Press), who first showed me Burckhardt; Alexsis and Jag Robertson, who helped me negotiate Saturn; Jehanne Mehta, who showed me a new way of loving; Marion Fawlk, for her affirmation and purity; Ferenc Aszmann, for his wit and radical integrity; Rae Beth, who confronted me with my shadow; Kristin Charlesworth, who helped me back to *rubedo*; Keith Casbon, for coming from another planet than my own; Susan Mears (my agent and friend), for her immaculate timing; Liz Puttick (my editor and friend), for her praise and faith that I could do it; Caroline Waterlow, who showed me the *prima materia*; Ted Partridge, for his wonderful golden lamp, and for 'being Ted'; Stanley Messenger, for his timely distillation; Judy de la Hoyde, who arrived with warm earth and cakes; Catherine Leonard and Marion Shiel, for their Irish breezes; Frances Emmelaus, for her royalty and for lending me *Mercurius*; Bob Moore (in Denmark), for his outstanding teaching; Christopher Johnson, for his penetrating healing; Niels Bandholm, for his precious loan of Fabricius; Maggie Peters, for being there at every turn of the dream; Richard Wainwright, for meeting me in the Queens; Mary Kingsley, for reminding me of the adventure; Lindsay Clarke, for being the red lion; Anne Baring and Robert Bly, for their eloquent support; Elizabeth Hutchins, for her demonic editing eye; Helen Elwes for her painstaking excellence in the nick of time ...

Also, all my client-companions and workshop participants in the Chrysalis community who have again and again demonstrated alchemy's relevance and reality to me through their process and their sharing; among them, especially Immaculate Manzi, Catherine Abbot, Emma Shackle and Sheila Ranger.

And above all to Lucy Lidell for her healing in Heaven and Earth, and for helping it come into actual form; and to Zanna Beswick, for showing me the end, and for her gift of gold in God on the way.

May we all go there, get there, be there – in the heart place where we know we belong.

J.R.

ONE

BEGINNING

*In a sense the secret of alchemy
is to imagine a world in which
it is possible to transmute
base metal to gold.*
PATRICK HARPUR

INTRODUCTION

Soror mystica – she raises her finger to her lips.

It may seem strange to begin by saying nothing, but the whole approach of this book is through feeling and imagination, and we have to be silent in order to feel. So I want to begin by offering you a short meditation exercise that is a key to the door of our subject:

Sit comfortably, read over what follows here and then lay it aside.

You will need some paper and a pen or pencil to write with.

Sitting quietly, just take a moment to be aware of your breathing, and as you breathe, slow down and deepen, breathing down into yourself.

Then begin to say the word ALCHEMY *inwardly, and allow it to resonate. Just keep repeating the word.*

What does it bring to mind?

How do you feel it in yourself, and where do you feel it?

And, staying with the word, where is it taking you to in your body?

What does it feel like there? Can you sense or see anything?

See if you can allow an image or a picture to come forward from that place to you, and trust what wants to come, whatever it is.

*Give yourself a moment to hold the image in your awareness ...
and then come back. Make a note of your image along with anything else that has come up for you during this exercise.*

Your experience here is your key: your core feeling and connection.

We are going to be doing other exercises like this as this work
proceeds. You might like to keep a journal as you read through
this book, not only to record what happens for you with the
exercises, but also to make this study your own, in your own
writing.

So why is alchemy important? Why does the word have such
power and depth? And what use is it to us now? Alchemy is a
process that involves the transmutation of base metal – or lead –
into gold, through a number of different stages that together
make up the 'Work', or 'Great Work'. It is both a literal or physical process and a metaphorical or inward one. It belongs to physical matter and to our feelings and imaginations. It belongs
inside our bodies, and to experiences we can't immediately understand, and we can see it happening outside in the world as
well. It is happening as we speak.

Alchemy is everywhere in our culture. Rock musicians have
named their albums after it – Dire Straits among them. The author and mystic Andrew Harvey has commented on it several
times in his *Dialogues with a Modern Mystic*, with American
journalist Mark Matousek; and Paulo Coelho's *The Alchemist*, a
fable about following your dreams, has been a bestseller since it
first came out in 1993. Lindsay Clarke's award-winning novel
The Chymical Wedding (1989) takes it as its central theme, as
does Patrick Harpur's alchemical journal-cum-novel *Mercurius*,
written at almost the same time. And the celebrated film-maker
and painter Derek Jarman was writing about it in June 1993, in
Chroma, a meditation on colour, one of his last books. It seems
that there is something very rich and deep to reclaim here.

Alchemy is unique in the Western Tradition for the way in which it brings spirit and matter together rather than separating them. It is profoundly non-dualistic in this sense, as opposed to the orthodox Christian Church, and also to alternative sects like the Gnostics and even the Cathars, who believed that matter was sinful or even evil – the realm of the pagan god Pan who became our image of the Devil. Alchemy holds no such belief, which is why it has always been radical, and heretical too, in terms of established thinking and morality.

Alchemy is also unique because of its emphasis on the individual person and the process involved in being an individual. Alchemists, traditionally, have been solitary workers – and the fruit of their labours has been their own experience and exploration. This is very different from the kind of attitude that creates dogma or a collective ideology of any kind. Alchemy denies such generalizing superficiality, although that hasn't prevented alchemists from being devout religious and spiritual people. In its conception and process, alchemy honours our individuality in every possible way.

Alchemy is also intensely creative, and we can understand and appreciate creativity more deeply through it, as well as having our own creativity stirred and stimulated by it. Alchemists who have compared notes, either with each other, or in retrospect across time, have found them the creative notes of a work-in-progress – a work that was and still is inexhaustible, and that lies at the heart of our inner evolution as imaginative and alive people. Alchemy appeals to our intuition and imagination rather than our intellect, because it is not a rational process: its logic is of a different order. As we say now it is *right* brain rather than left brain. Alchemists were in fact pioneers of the unconscious – a term we take for granted today – long before psychotherapy as such came into being or therapy became available. Alchemy speaks to our dreaming mind, to our unconscious, where we see with the eyes of the soul, and so I have called it 'a path of the soul'. It illuminates our soul-being in its inner workings, so we learn to see by a deeper light.

As Kat Duff describes it, from her own experience, in *The Alchemy of Illness*:

> Then one day, as I stood in my kitchen stirring powdered vitamin C into a glass of water, staring at the vast array of medicinal bottles on the counter, I realized that my illness and its healing were matters of chemistry. That chemistry was very physical, as in the magnesium and potassium I took to help my body assimilate the vitamin C, but there was something more to it, for there were times when remedies worked, or did not work, for no apparent reason. For example, I often felt better as soon as I swallowed my vitamin C, long before it had time to take effect. Medical researchers call it the 'placebo effect'; I prefer to call it magic, for it occurs when something – a pill or a word – is imbued with power and meaning, and so becomes more effective. That is alchemy.[1]

Alchemy is vibrant: it reaches to the source of life. Another aspect of its relevance now is its inclusion of sexuality as part of the dynamic between the masculine and feminine aspects of the process. I shall be concentrating on this in the main part of this book. Alchemy's understanding of sexuality is radical. Sex is not just sex: it is depth, it is dying, it is purification and it is redemption. Within it, alchemy points to our true being as men and women – as kings and queens – and as well as honouring our potential there, in its emphasis on androgyny in the figure of the bisexual hermaphrodite, it points to as yet unexplored areas of gender. It also suggests that we each have *unique* gender as expressions of the masculine and feminine within us, and it is in this too that alchemy offers us profound healing at a time when we are so blatantly sexually wounded and confused.

As Smith, vicar by day and alchemist in his basement at night, says in *Mercurius*:

All this was in my mind as I walked in the moonlit wood, and I was afraid. Never has our Philosophy been more needed. Never has Spirit been such a scarce commodity. It must be sought out in that quarter where it is least expected – in matter. Only our Philosophy can retrieve it from the shadowy subterranean kingdom; only our Art ceases to look vainly to the vast Above and begins ... with the Below.[2]

Above all, alchemy is about wholeness – about the whole of who we are, and about living whole rather than partial and suppressed lives. Wholeness, by definition, means inclusion rather than denial, or, as Carole Bruce, photographer and therapist, once said to me, 'All denial is a denial of God.' Alchemy argues that everything is a part of God, otherwise it wouldn't exist. And since it exists, it is part of the Work.

Wholeness here also means looking at what we haven't lived: at what is in the shadow of who we think we are, or who we have so far been. And this is where the potency of alchemy lies, because in that recognition is a place where we can no longer escape ourselves, a place of confrontation where the Work, and the process it entails, begins.

But the wholeness that alchemy challenges us to is also about expansion – expanding our minds and hearts, becoming more largely ourselves and more a part of Creation. It is a process that invites us to stay the course of our lives and understand, in that, why we actually live as long as we do, however long that is for each of us. As one workshop participant remarked during a day introduction I ran at the College of Psychic Studies in London, 'You know, I think this kind of thing has been happening to me all my life.'

Alchemy takes time, as love takes time and gold takes time. It isn't a quick fix – as every alchemist knows, it requires forbearance and patience, and more patience, as we recognize that the timing is not simply our own.

Alchemy's work of making Heaven on Earth turns us both inward and outwards at the same time: we live more deeply in our world as well as see more completely where we are as part of the larger cosmic picture. What alchemy – and Smith's 'our Philosophy' – stands for here, then, is not only knowledge but also wisdom: knowledge learnt and suffered through experience. This is its promise in the symbol of the Seal of Solomon, where the upward-pointing triangle of soul and substance, and the downward-pointing triangle of spirit and essence merge and become a star:

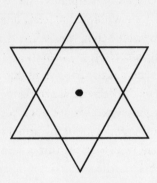

So, having glimpsed the end, ahead of time, let us now look at the beginning in terms of what alchemy is. For we need to know what it is, to *feel* what it is, before we can begin to use it. At this point you might want to take a moment to reconnect to your initial mediation exercise (*see p.3*). Can you see a connection?

Stanislaus Klossowski de Rola has described alchemy[3] as 'a hidden reality of the highest order'. I think that's a very useful and precise phrase, and I'd draw your attention to the words 'hidden' and 'highest' here, placed side by side. There is a sense of height and depth simultaneously, which is in every way appropriate. As a *philosophy* – and as a cosmology, to do with sun, moon and stars – alchemy is a bridge between Earth and Heaven, matter and spirit, the solid and the fluid, the visible and the invisible, bringing the horizontal and the vertical together.

As a *process*, as already mentioned, alchemy involves the transmutation of base metal into gold *during which consciousness is
radically altered* – that is, the consciousness of the alchemist, or
artifex as he or she was called. In this case, it is you and I.

Alchemy is a physical process to do with self-knowledge, then;
and again, we can't have access to that knowledge without being
in touch with the body and the ground: our earth.

Overall, the process that the Great Work, or *Magnum Opus*,
represents consists of two major phases that correspond to what
alchemists call 'the Lesser Work' (*nigredo* and *solutio*) and 'the
Greater Work' (*coagulatio* and *rubedo*). These have to do respectively with *the spiritualization of the body* and then *the embodiment of spirit*. You can reflect on this physically by imagining
the spiritualization of the body as a gesture upwards, perhaps of
raising the palms of your hands above your head, and then a gesture downwards, down and in, that brings the whole sense of
your energy down and into your body as you stand.

*You might like to take a moment to simply stand and do this. Be
aware of the gestures you find yourself making and the relationship
between them, moving up and then down.*

As above, so below:
As within, so without.

These two major phases of the Work, or *opus*, in turn have to do
with two aspects, as alchemists all agree.

The first involves a mastery over the *prima materia*, or 'first
matter', as they call it, which means the raw stuff or chaos both
in ourselves and in our lives.

The second involves, correspondingly, and as a result of going
through the process, what is called 'the inward creation of a body
of light' that relates to consciousness, the gold and, in terms of
the body, resurrection: literally, new life.

Derek Jarman lists the stages:

BLACK:
The base material was the prima materia, *a chaos like the*
dark waters of the deep. Melanosis and nigredo.

WHITE:
The cleansing calcined albedo.

YELLOW:
Another stage, xanthosis.

PURPLE:
Iosis, *the colour of kingship.*
Pursuing the goal you crossed that Red Sea.[4]

Alchemy is a journey of dying and being born or reborn. In modern terms this translates into a journey from the ego-state or 'me-state' to the Self – the 'I' that I truly am, my true being and identity. The Red Sea that Derek Jarman alludes to points to the nature of the terrain that lies in between: a strange and miraculous country that is submerged in fire and water, like our bellies, where we can only see by moonlight and the soles of our feet on the ground …

Another important clue for us here at the beginning of our journey into alchemy lies in the word itself. Its origin is in Arabic: *al kimia*, variously translated as 'the black soil art' or 'the Egyptian art', in relationship to the Egyptian word *chem* meaning 'black' and also to the Greek word *chyma* which designates the casting or fusing of metals. It has also been related to the Hebrew word *chamaman*, meaning 'a mystery' in the sense of something occult or secret, not easily revealed. This is certainly in keeping with its nature as well as its history.

Let us now look briefly at the core text or revelation that lies at the heart of alchemy – *The Emerald Tablet* (*Tabula smaragdina*), which is attributed to Hermes Trismegistus. The legend is that Sarah, the wife of Abraham in the Bible, took it from his dead hands and Alexander the Great later discovered it in the cave where his tomb was. Hermes Trismegistus (meaning 'three times powerful' or 'thrice born') is both a priestly archetype and a father figure – and in a very real sense every alchemist is a descendant of his, just as we are all said to come from Adam. Emerald, the colour of the heart, applied in Graeco-Egyptian times to any green stone. Who the actual author was remains unknown and there are various translations of the text. The oldest is in Arabic, others (including the version here) are from Latin. It is a memorable as well as beautiful piece of writing, really like a prose-poem, and I suggest you read it several times for yourself before we turn to something of what it means:

The Emerald Tablet

1. *In truth certainly and without doubt whatever is below is like that which is above, and whatever is above is like that which is below, to accomplish the miracles of one thing.*
2. *Just as all things proceed from One alone by meditation on One alone, so also they are born from this one thing by adaptation.*
3. *Its father is the sun and its mother is the moon. The wind has borne it in its body. Its nurse is the earth.*
4. *It is the father of every miraculous work in the whole world.*
5. *Its power is perfect if it is converted into earth.*
6. *Separate the earth from the fire and the subtle from the gross, softly and with great prudence.*
7. *It rises from earth to heaven and comes down again from heaven to earth, and thus acquires the power of the realities above and the realities below. In this way you will acquire the glory of the whole world, and all darkness will leave you.*

8. *This is the power of all powers, for it conquers everything subtle and penetrates everything solid.*
9. *Thus the little world is created according to the prototype of the great world.*
10. *From this and in this way, marvellous applications are made.*
11. *For this reason I am called Hermes Trismegistus, for I possess the three parts of wisdom of the whole world.*
12. *Perfect is what I have said of the work of the sun.*

TRANSLATED BY J. F. RUSKA[5]

'As above, so below': this is where the saying originates, and it points to the connection I've already made between Heaven and Earth, that is also the 'great world' and the 'little world' in verse 9. The 'miracles of one thing' (in verse 1) refers here to the Work or process, which takes place because of this connection. As for its 'father' and its 'mother' (verse 3), we will be looking at the significance of sun and moon with Sol and Luna later, but this is also meant cosmically – and astrologically as well, alchemists believe. The 'wind' (verse 3) is the breath, and inspiration, too – the word means 'to breathe in' – and its 'nurse' is the body: our individual bodies as well. Its 'father' as the sun places the sun centrally and the sun also refers to the gold as a state of supreme clarity that is also a circle, as the sun is.

And now, in verse 5, we have the statement that refers to the Greater Work or the embodiment of Spirit: 'Its power is perfect ...' – literally meaning that *it works* 'if it is converted into earth'. This is what it promises.

Verses 6 and 7 go on to allude to the internal transformatory process as well as what happens inside the alchemist's heated flask, and link to the core saying of our subject which is *solve et coagula*, literally 'dissolve and re-form', or die and be re-born. Then through this 'all darkness' – in the sense of grossness, ignorance and stupidity as well as illusion – 'will leave you'.

Then it proclaims that 'this is the power of all powers'; in other words, the strongest energy there is, is the truth. This is the strongest place to be, however vulnerable it might make us.

And so the statement in verse 9 follows, the truth that lies at the heart of Creation itself – if we could but see it. If we can, then miracles can take place as we live in the light of it – the light that is the sun, the gold, and famous philosopher's Stone. All these are synonyms for truth.

In verse 11, then, we have another meaning for 'Trismegistus' – as an initiated state of being where the 'three parts of wisdom', brought together, are Spirit, psyche (or soul), and body in a wholeness that is 'the whole world'. We can understand this wholeness as a healed and healing state as well.

And the work of the sun? Is perfect, then. It works, as the text says, as it comes full circle. And we can read it again and again, the more we begin to know.

Take a moment now to simply sit and imagine the sun for a moment directly in front of your forehead, until you can feel the light from it coming into you … being aware of how you feel as it does.

You can do this in actual sunlight, too.

The Emerald Tablet is not an easy text, but it does prepare us for the difficulties we encounter in alchemical language, as well as being in itself a key to other writings that are far more obscure and impenetrable.

To get a deeper grounding in it, we need to turn to some of the history of alchemy. This is also another way of introducing some of the more important ideas before we go into the process itself.

So now, some essential history.

TWO

A BRIEF HISTORY

Shall all men teache?
What manner of people may this science reache,
And which is the true science of alchemis
Of ould fathers called blessed and holi?

THOMAS NORTON, ORDINALL OF ALKIMIE

If it is profitable to understand nature in human terms, alchemy
has a present value; if not, it can interest us only as history.

F. SHERWOOD-TAYLOR

You ask me to summarize for you in four minutes four thousand years of philosophy and the efforts of a life-time. Further-
more, you ask me to translate into ordinary language concepts
for which such a language is not intended ...

FULCANELLI, QUOTED BY JACQUES BERGIER

A BRIEF HISTORY

Above, text:
below, the river

The roots of alchemy are complex and deep. They reach and trail down into the earth, and back in time, spanning seas and continents. The history of alchemy is in the ground, in the earth where it came from and where it still is now. It is like a Tree of Life reaching down, the way roots reach trailing for nutrients.

Alchemy has always been referred to as the 'Divine Art' or 'Sacred Art', and until the fifth century AD that is what it was known as. While our concern here is with the Western Tradition, alchemy reaches back into China, before 2500 BC, and subsequently into India and the Far East, encompassing Japan and South East Asia. In both China and India, it was specifically to do with longevity – with prolonging human life. We find this in both the Chinese word *Chin-jo* ('gold juice' or 'elixir') and in the Indian Tantras, which are a section of the *Vedas*, the oldest sacred writings in their tradition. But we need to go deeper still to find the common source. That lies in a way of looking at the earth as a magical and living entity, a Gaia of its own source, a buried jewel lined with layers and veins of ore where minerals and metals grow. We have moved very far away from this view now and we need to recover that sense of reverence – the primitive reverence we had that permeates the 'sacred task' of the early smiths.[1]

The same attitude surfaces throughout alchemical writing. Here is Valentinus, for example, another legendary figure – possibly a Benedictine monk – writing in the fifteenth century:

All herbs, trees, and roots, and all metals and minerals, receive their growth and nutriment from the spirit of the earth, which is the spirit of life. This spirit is itself fed by the stars, and is thereby rendered capable of imparting nutriment to all things that grow and of nursing them as a mother does her child while it is yet in her womb. The minerals are hidden in the womb of the earth and nourished by her with the spirit that she receives from above.[2]

Again we can see here the connection between the earth and the stars that is being forged in a very physically real way, that is at the same time subtle and invisible, or 'hidden'. It is in this understanding of matter and energy that we can begin to appreciate what alchemists mean by the earth.

ANCIENT

The recorded beginnings of alchemy are in Egypt, and the earliest alchemists, although writing in Greek, were Egyptian and Jewish. The foremost among these, and the Mother of Alchemy on a practical and earthly level, is Maria Prophetissa, in legend the sister of Moses, and also known as Mary the Jewess. From her we have the saying that directly foreshadows the stages of the process:

One becomes two, two becomes three, and out of the third comes the one as the fourth.

She has another saying, too, about marrying 'the white and the red gum' i.e. the fourth stage that is *rubedo*. She was also responsible for inventing both the still and the retort as part of the basic laboratory apparatus. She points to the existence of other women alchemists (like Zosimus' sister Theosebeia) as well.

The other well known name here, after Democritus, is Zosimus, a fifth-century laboratory worker, visionary and prolific writer of treatises, including *The Great and Divine Art of the Making of Gold and Silver*. Other alchemical 'writers' like Iamblicus, Moses and even Cleopatra, are, however, certainly fictitious. Ascribing texts to them was simply an attempt to gain authority and credibility for the subject. An ancient and famous author commanded more respect than someone who was, often enough, an unknown contemporary.

What we see with these earliest practitioners is this sense of ground and earth as well as the foundation of alchemy as an experimental science. Alchemy begins here literally as a physical process: a laboratory process where the main concern was with the artificial making of gold and silver and sometimes precious gem stones, with techniques that survive in modern jewellery-making. This was largely achieved by the colouring effect of alloys; for instance, the 'whitening' of copper (using arsenic) and the 'yellowing' (using polysulphides gained by boiling lime and sulphur), heated at high temperatures.

The most successful experiments, for which some eccentric and wacky recipes remain, were for the 'doubling of gold' (literally, making twice or more the quantity). Out of this two primary ideas of importance emerge. The first is of gold 'tested by fire' – which was the test of its quality – and the second was the belief that gold as a seed or ferment was capable of transmuting a mass of base metal into itself. We need to take these metaphorically as well as literally.

At the same time, with the development of laboratory equipment and the process of distillation as well as calcination (burning), with the 'blackening' (lead residue), the 'whitening' and the 'yellowing', three of the main stages of the Work came into being. And in the process itself? What could these early alchemists have felt as they watched a metal become a black formless mass, and then a metal again – in fact a more glorious metal in their eyes?

From black to gold: death and resurrection, metal molten in its fluid light silent with meaning ...

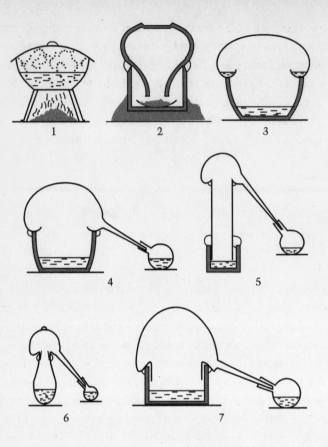

In this connection too comes the ancient parallel between alchemy and astrology, between the planets and their associated metals, which predates Egypt and Greece. So the cosmic picture, centring on the Sun, takes shape:

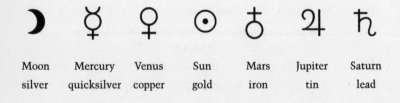

Moon	Mercury	Venus	Sun	Mars	Jupiter	Saturn
silver	quicksilver	copper	gold	iron	tin	lead

Saturn, then, was the outermost planet (preceding the discovery of Neptune, Uranus, Pluto and most recently, Chiron), and with the other planets ringed like a spiral, there is *an inward movement to the centre* that is the Sun/gold, the Sun-gold as centre: the dot in the circle's centre:

MEDIEVAL

This period sees alchemy coming to the West. The first translations were made from Arabic texts – notably from Jabir-ibn-Hayyan, or Geber as he became known in Europe – and these included *The Emerald Tablet*. Alchemy had permeated Islamic culture from the eighth century as a result of Arab involvement in Egypt and the Arabs brought it in turn to Spain and southern Italy. The first known translation of an Arabic alchemical text into English was made by Robert of Chester, while he was in Spain, in 1144.

Interest in the subject began to grow in an atmosphere of scientific awakening, and the keenest minds of the day – among them Albertus Magnus, Roger Bacon and Thomas Aquinas – were involved. Was alchemy real? Did it come from God? Could it really do what it claimed? Pope John XII thought not and a papal edict condemning it was passed in 1317:

Poor themselves, the alchemists promise riches which are not forthcoming; wise also in their own conceit, they fall into the ditch which they themselves have digged.

Others, like Albertus Magnus, saw differently – and in his precepts for the alchemist we can begin to see how alchemists came to be set apart from society:

First. *He should be discreet and silent, revealing to no one the result of his operations.*
Second. *He should reside in a private house in an isolated position.*
Third. *He should choose his days and hours for labour with discretion.*
Fourth. *He should have patience, diligence, and perseverance.*
Fifth. *He should perform according to fixed rules.*
Sixth. *He should use only vessels of glass or glazed earthenware.*
Seventh. *He should be sufficiently rich to bear the expenses of his art.*
Eighth. *He should avoid having anything to do with princes and noblemen.*[3]

That last warning, as we will see, was ignored by some with fatal consequences.

The medieval mind brought in a quality of argument and precision; so we see the process being presented in a more ordered as well as a more cosmological way. A fine example of this is in the writings attributed to Ramon Lull (d.1316), one of the most influential philosophers of the time.

Lull introduces us to what came to be known as the *prima materia*: the 'first matter'. He proposed it as *argent vive*, literally 'living silver' or quicksilver, in fact mercury – which, as we will see, in relationship to Hermes or Mercurius, is the essence of the process.

Lull argued that this was the original substance out of which everything else in Creation came. The finest part formed the bodies of the angels, then the heavenly spheres, stars and planets, and then the coarser part the terrestrial or earthly bodies; our own included. In matter, this *argent vive* became the four elements: fire, earth, air and water – with a part remaining separate: the fifth element he called the *quintessence*. So, in other words, he was saying that a part of the heavenly is in everything and that, as a result, divine influence can bring about generation and corruption, or death and rebirth, in us.

This argument or vision is drawn from the *Testament of Lullius*,[4] which spread after his martyr's death when he was stoned by Moslems on arriving in Africa. It is pure alchemical cosmology and can speak to us in our time as well. The heavenly and the earthly are interfused together in it:

Argent Vive
heavenly bodies: angels
heavenly spheres
quintessence
fire, earth, air and water
Man/Woman
trees, plants, minerals, rocks
– terra firma.

At the same time, the physical base of alchemy continued in relationship to this in the discovery of alcohol, as distilled from wine (called *aqua ardens*; 'a water which would burn'), alongside the belief in it as a quintessence and its subsequent use as a medicine – for instance, with Benedictine, invented by Dom Bernardo Vincelli in 1510. Alcohol itself was also discovered to have the ability to extract herbal and plant essences – their quintessence, in other words – so the healing dimension of alchemy begins to emerge with the origin of the flower remedies we know today.

'As above, so below.' So there was progress on both fronts. And the more that Heaven is explored, the more Earth can reveal itself – if we have an eye for it. Alchemists do, and did.

Yet, just as light always has its shadow, so the pure-minded alchemist is accompanied by a con man. This 'impure' or 'false' alchemy also emerges at this time and continues over the three centuries that follow, as alchemy became all the rage. The alchemical con man (interestingly enough, no women are recorded here) dresses, or rather *overdresses*, for the part and succeeds in extracting money out of gullible patrons among the wealthy with a variety of fairly basic conjuring tricks. These centred on a demonstration where an experiment was set up with a furnace and a crucible filled with mercury where the precious 'powder of prejection' (the substance of the Stone) was introduced – either as a little chalk or red lead – and the mixture heated. Meanwhile, of course, some gold had been secreted inside a piece of charcoal or at the end of a stirring rod. The heated mercury evaporated, leaving, apparently, a button of pure gold. Other tricks of the trade included using a nail or knife that was already half gold, but coated in black, which a solvent removed for the audience's satisfaction.

The pseudo-alchemists, or 'puffers' as they came to be called (because of the bellows they used to inflate their egos), were satirized from the beginning by Geoffrey Chaucer in his *Canon's Yeoman's Tale*[5] – and later, most famously, by Ben Jonson in his play *The Alchemist* (1610). But that didn't stop them coming. The interesting thing, as various stories about them tell, is that they rarely got away with it – and the penalties included torture as well as imprisonment, public disgrace and death. It is almost as if alchemy has its own inbuilt punishment for the betrayal of its spirit. But the pseudo-alchemists, unconscious as they were, do reveal the problems of the chemical process itself. We'll come on to that later.

There is no such problem, though, with the French alchemist Nicholas Flamel (1330–1417) and his wife Perenelle. Flamel, who worked as a scrivener (a writer or drafter of documents) in Paris, met alchemy in the form of a large gilded book he bought, supposedly written by Abraham Eleazar, which contained a number of fascinating but baffling illustrations with some obscure text, possibly Greek. The illustrations included pictures of a virgin being swallowed by snakes, a crucified snake, and a wilderness region with fountains and snakes in it. What did all this mean? Flamel consulted Anselm, a medicinal friend, who couldn't really help. He then experimented for years to find out himself – without success – before going on a pilgrimage to Spain in the hope of finding a rabbi who could help him (Eleazar being Jewish). That was no use either, until on his way back he briefly met a Master Canches, in Lyon. Canches interpreted the illustrations for Flamel with joy – it is said – but then died on the journey back to Paris, leaving Flamel alone. Returning, Flamel set to work and, after three years, so we are told, succeeded in making the 'first agent' on 17 January, 1392. He recognized it by its strong smell. In the presence of his wife he then transmuted half a pound of mercury into pure silver. Then, on 25 April, he made a projection of the red stone on the same amount of mercury, turning it to pure gold. He then repeated the experiment three times.

As a result, he and Perenelle became hugely wealthy, but rather than keeping their riches for themselves, founded hospitals, built chapels, endowed churches and restored cemeteries. They used their gold, on other words, in service to the world as king and queen. Perenelle, we can imagine, accompanied Flamel's labours not only as wife, but also as his lover and *soror mystica*, the mystical sister or guiding feminine presence that helps a man find himself, in the depths of his own heart, alone, in silence.

In every detail of his story, Nicholas Flamel was that rare thing – a *true* alchemist.

'Renaissance' literally means 'rebirth' or 'renewal' and in the period between the fourteenth and sixteenth centuries we find this impulse affecting every branch of intellectual and creative expression in Europe. At this time, painting, sculpture, poetry, theology and philosophy, inspired by classicism, all reached forward and broke new ground.

Central in this for alchemy were the translations of the Greek alchemical, or Hermetic, texts by Marsilio Ficino in Italy. And as well as affirming alchemy as an experimental discipline, Renaissance writers saw the opportunity of combining natural magic with Christian theology in a new and exciting synthesis.

Two outstanding figures of importance emerge during this time, both of them German. The first is Cornelius Agrippa (1486–1535), whose *Occult Philosophy*, with its blend of Neoplatonism, magic and Cabbala, became a handbook for the new thinking. In it – in line with Ramon Lull – he identifies three main levels of being: the lowest world he describes as the 'elements' and linked to natural magic; the astral realm, in which he includes mathematics; and the angelic realm of 'angel magic', which includes access to the intelligence of higher beings. Finally he asserts 'the name of Jesus, now all-powerful, [contains] the powers of the Tetragrammaton' (or original name of God). Just as with Flamel, there is a Christian emphasis which is more than just a simple assertion of blind faith.

Agrippa tried everything in his wandering life and was critical of alchemists as 'either physicians or soap-boilers'. In the *Vanity of Sciences and Arts*, his last book, he paints a picture of failure around the alchemist that was perhaps also his own:

> When he expects the reward of his labours, births of gold, youth, and immortality, after all his time and expense, at length old, ragged, rich only in misery, and so miserable that he will sell his soul for three farthings, he falls upon ill courses and counterfeiting of money ...[6]

Like Jonathan Swift, he ends up castigating everything with an ashy eye – and yet his philosophy remains alchemical as well as innovative.

The second important figure is Paracelsus (d.1541), who approaches the issue differently. His whole argument is that alchemy is not about making gold – or at least, material gold – but is instead to produce medicine. As a Renaissance doctor, Paracelsus was a one-man revolution. He overturned the tables of the medical past, decrying the doctors of his day with their academic practices as 'painted monkeys', primitive in the extreme, and instead advocated plunging into what he called 'the Book of Nature', in other words, actual research experience and the alchemy of the natural world. He even burnt the books of the fathers of medicine publicly at one of his lectures as Professor at Basle University. This action, which resulted in the loss of his job, wasn't merely anarchic – it was in the name of his spiritual convictions. As he said:

> God makes the true physician, but not without pains on man's part ...[7]

For Paracelsus, who studied alchemy in his youth with Trithemius, Abbot of Sponheim, the essence of Nature or of natural law was defined by the relationship between the three principles of mercury, sulphur and salt. Sulphur and mercury, or quicksilver, create the dynamic central to the process itself. Beyond that, God for Paracelsus was not an Old Testament figure with a white beard, but what he called the *Mysterium Magnum*, the Great Mystery, a way of seeing that is closer to the Holy Spirit in its formless sense of all-embracing permeation and wonder. Again, this is not a dualistic view. Paracelsus argued, that as part of the earth and the stars, we each have an *inner* heavenly being, or *astra* – which is where we get the term 'astral body' – and it is *that*, he claims, which governs our health and sickness. Paracelsus believed that if the body displayed imbalance, then chemical medicine was necessary. At the same time, the remedies he invented and worked with were based on the idea of quintessence, as already described. So, in contemporary terms, he was working with a complementary approach that was both allopathic and homoeopathic. It was holistic: he was seeking to treat and heal the whole person.

Paracelsus' impact, like his personality, was charismatic and enormous, and his work – including his *Astronomia magna* (1537-9) – is still being studied and annotated all these centuries later. His philosophy is the most consistent of any alchemical practitioner, and his mysticism and second sight are second to none. Like Agrippa, he was a wanderer and died in poverty. But what he leaves us with outlives us all: as he said, *we are stardust*.

IN ENGLAND

Meanwhile, here in England, alchemy was widespread and people from every class were involved in the craze: gentry, tradesmen, priests, monks and laity. As Thomas Norton observed in his *Ordinall*, written in 1477:

> *Common workmen will not be out-lafte*
> *For as well as Lords they love this noble craft*

and as a result – partly to separate the wheat from the chaff – statutes were issued against 'the multiplication of metals'. Thereafter licenses had to be bought in order to practise alchemy, many still chose to break the law. As an anonymous writer warned:

> *Therefore keep close of thy tongue and of thy hand*
> *From the officers and governors of the land;*
> *And from other men that they of thy craft nothing know*
> *For in witness thereof they will thee hang and draw.*[8]

This raises the whole issue of secrecy, not only in relationship to the systems of signs and symbols that alchemical texts are littered with (originally as a protection against the uninitiated), but also – with that emphasis still very much in place – for practical reasons, remembering what Albertus Magnus counselled (*see p.22*). Anyone who could reasonably be supposed to be able to make gold was liable to be asked, or even forced, to try and do so, and there is evidence of this from the time of Edward III onwards, right through to Queen Elizabeth I, and Charles I and Charles II in the seventeenth century. Alchemists were particularly vulnerable. Not only were they dealing in a difficult and complex quest for which no one had any single right answer; but now they were also prey to those who wanted to swell their bank accounts.

Some of them tried – and others were actually victimized. Norton tells the story of Thomas Daulton (d.1471), 'a good man' as he says, who was brought before Edward IV by one of his squires, Lord Herbert. Sir John Delves, whom Daulton had worked for, broke his oath of secrecy in telling the king that Daulton 'had made him a thousand pounds of good gold in less than a day'. Daulton then told the king that he had thrown the red powder (or Stone) into a lake to avoid more trouble. The king released him, but then Lord Herbert kidnapped him, taking him to his own castle in Monmouthshire where he tried to get the secret out of him, keeping him imprisoned there for four years. But Daulton wouldn't tell.

Daulton died soon after his release, from the strain of his imprisonment. As Norton drily observes:

> This was his payne as I you tell
> By men who had no dread of hell.
> Herbert died soon after in his bedd
> And Delves at Tewkesbury lost his head.

Under such circumstances, it's little wonder that the story at the heart of alchemy is one of difficulty and obscurity, even though progress was still being made.

There were real and honest masters, however, Norton himself among them. Born in Bristol, he is famous for his main work the

Ordinall of Alchimie, the long alchemical poem I've been quoting from, which is full of history and valuable information as well as permeated with religious feeling and commitment. His own commitment involved him in riding for 100 miles to find his master (who may have been George Ripley), and spending 40 days learning the art.

George Ripley (d. circa 1490), was a Canon at Bridlington in Yorkshire. He attempted a clearer description of all the stages of the process in his *Compound of Alchymie* (1475) where he names them as a series of 12 gates: Calcination, Solution, Separation, Conjunction, Putrefaction, Congelation, Cibation, Sublimation, Fermentation, Exaltation, Multiplication and Projection.[9]

Meeting with a master was vital, as the art was passed on by word of mouth. The story goes that Ripley passed it on to 'a Canon of Lichfield' who in turn gave it to Thomas Daulton, while William Holloweye (alias Gibbs), Prior of Bath Abbey, passed it to Thomas Charnock (b. 1524), who practised it in Combwich, a small village in Somerset.

Charnock tells us more about the trials of being an alchemist. He relates the difficulty of keeping the work secret and the curiosity of the various craftsmen involved in making the necessary apparatus. We can imagine the potter or the glassmaker asking, 'What would you want *that* for?' Then there was the expense of it all – before the actual work could even begin. And once it had? Charnock's story is a moving tale of frustration, failure and renewed attempts which included him smashing the whole laboratory up with a hatchet in a rage when he was forced to leave it for the siege of Calais. Even at the end of his life, in 1581, after endless 'circulations', he was still trying to make the white stone.[10]

A hundred years later, a neighbouring clergyman reports:

I saw on the dore of his little Athanor-room (if I may so call it) drawne by his owne hand, with coarse colours and worke but ingeniously, an Embleme of the Worke, at which I gave some

guesses, and soe about the walls in his Chamber, I think there
was in all 5 panes of his works, all somewhat differing from
each other, some very obscure and almost worne out.

    They told me that people had been unwilling to dwell in
that house, because reputed troublesome, I presume from
some traditionall stories, of this person, who was looked on by
his Neighbours as no better than a Conjuror ...[11]

Here we see the social situation of the alchemist – in many ways
so like an artist, only worse – in graphic detail.

But within this, and within the evolving understanding of the
Work, what we see is an increasing *humanization* of the process.
This is absolutely vital to our understanding of it, to what alchemy itself becomes, and to what it has to give us now. As their
imaginations were fired and stirred, alchemists were drawing on
analogies from human life to describe what they saw taking place
chemically. F. Sherwood-Taylor, whose historical work on alchemy is profound and penetrating, puts it as well as anyone can:

The combination of two bodies he saw as a marriage, *the loss*
of their characteristic activity as death, *the production of*
something new, as a birth, *the rising up of vapours, as a* spirit
leaving the corpse, the formation of a volatile solid, as the
making of a spiritual body. *These conceptions influenced his*
idea of what should occur, and he therefore decided that the
final end of the substances operated on should be analogous to
the final end of man – a soul in a new, glorious body, with the
qualities of clarity, subtlety, and agility.[12]

As a result of this, the main characters in the drama of the
process are introduced. We will be looking at and working with
each of these in more detail in the main body of this book. They
are:

the Old King
(or old state of consciousness)

Sol
(the sun, sulphur: the masculine principle)

Luna
(the moon, quicksilver: the feminine principle)

Mercurius
(= Hermes, mercury: the chief agent of the process and the
hermaphrodite/bisexual/androgynous principle)

Lady Alchymia
(sometimes called *Anima Mercurii*: the Spirit of alchemy and its
guiding presence and initiator)

the alchemist himself or herself
(or *artifex*)

the *soror mystica* or *frater mysterium*
(the mystical sister or secret brother: his or her companion in
the Work)

Each of these is portrayed in many different ways – in as many
ways as they are individually conceived and imagined.

This introduces another area of importance and that is the alchemical pictures or images which often illustrate key texts, as
with the book Nicholas Flamel discovered. They reach a sub-
lime level in illustrated editions like the *Splendor solis* (1582).[13]
These pictures, some of which are reproduced throughout this
book, came into being because of the difficulty alchemists found
in expressing their understanding in words. There is no doubt,
too, that they also preserved something of the secrecy of the art
– and were intended for that purpose – but either way, we can
see that the visual language of alchemy is just as important as

its verbal expression, and is sometimes more accessible. The pictures, which range from crude sketches to full-blown paintings, invite us to imagine, to move from our rational to our intuitive capacity. Dream-like, they are images from the unconscious or from the soul's own light, and yet they are also deliberate, conscious expressions. Alchemical pictures and images are the first art form of the unconscious, long before either Surrealism or Expressionism, and they have never, as far as I know, been exhibited. But we can certainly understand more about an artist like William Blake, for instance, as a result of studying them, for he illustrated his poems with engravings in a not so different way.[14]

But above all, these images of dragons, lions, snakes, ravens, pelicans, skeletons, suns and moons, Sol and Luna, king and queen, and the ever-present Mercurius are a call to our own expression of what we feel in the depths of our own physical being.

So I want to suggest now that you have a look at some of them through the pages of this book – and sense if you can the feelings they evoke in you.

What are they?

Fascination? Repulsion? Confusion?

What is your physical response to them?

And then close your eyes for a moment or two and see what comes to mind ...

HERMETIC

Perhaps the climax of English alchemy is in the Renaissance figure of John Dee, with his vast library in Mortlake (now a suburb of London) which included a whole section on Paracelsus, his main influence, and his laboratory. As well as practising alchemy and astrology, Dee taught cosmography, travelled to Europe to the famous 'Gold Alley' in Prague seeking audience with the Emperor Rudolf II and, in the 1580s, held séances of 'angel magic'. These produced a series of remarkable transmissions, including

The 48 Angelic Keys which predict some of what has been happening in our Aquarian Age by nearly four centuries.

But if Dee, with his complex personality, was successful and charismatic, he was also one of the last of his kind, because from the beginning of the seventeenth century, when he died, alchemy becomes something increasingly inward, with the emphasis firmly away from showmanship or publicity of any kind.

'Hermetic', which derives from Hermes, literally means 'secret' or 'sealed' – sealed from the outside, a condition that is vital for the process, which takes place 'in the flask'. The term also contains the idea that this is something you can only understand by being *inside* it, just as we can only understand love when we are *in* love. Alchemy requires the same inwardness and privacy, the same sealed or sacred space.

The other reason for this has to do with the rise of chemistry, specifically after 1650, when science and the rational 'Enlightenment' (so called) began to gain ground. Increasingly, the chemical aspect of alchemy passed to the chemists. So what happened to alchemy? It became spiritualized. From this time onward, alchemy takes on the preservation of a world view which is Divine as opposed to one which separated mind and matter in the service of analysis, one without a spiritual perspective. So alchemy begins to leave the literal dimension of the laboratory and becomes philosophy – Hermetic Philosophy. And with that new emphasis, a new challenge opens, which points ahead towards where we are now. Alchemy offers us *the science of ourselves*.

We see this in the work of the German mystic and shoemaker Jakob Boehme (d.1624), also influenced by Paracelsus, who saw into the heart of 'the Book of Nature' and called the Stone the 'Spirit of Christ'. We see it with the work of Michael Maier (d.1622), another German, who practised as a doctor and was involved with the Rosicrucians, and we see it with Robert Fludd (d.1637), an English physician who, with his huge work *The History of the Microcosm and the Macrocosm*, wove all the alternative strands of thought together. And we also see it with Thomas Vaughan (1621–65), twin brother of the metaphysical poet Henry

Vaughan and contemporary of John Donne, who significantly describes literal alchemy as a 'torture of metals':

> I have, Reader, in several little Tractats delivered my judgement of philosophie, for Alchymie in the common acceptation, as it is a torture of Metalls, I did never believe, much less did I study it.[15]

So what is Hermetic Philosophy in essence? It is Neoplatonist and it is Christian, too, though not the kind of Christianity we would normally recognize. In many ways it is like Ramon Lull's philosophy (see pp.22–3), with a greater number of influences from the Renaissance.

Again, the essential idea is holistic, bringing 'above' and 'below' together as a consequence of the Divine, or God. As a trinity of Father (or Father–Mother), Son and Holy Ghost, we can structure it like this:

SUN

God: as supernatural foundation

Light

God the Son: in whose image things are made

Fire

God the Holy Ghost: the spirit framing the Creation

– and God, as the *Mysterium Magnum* or Great Mystery, is simultaneously *all* of this: unnameable, beyond them and within them as the Source and the Secret.

The hermetic alchemists saw God as having created the 'first matter' – and in their idea of Genesis this was the darkness, the blackness that the Light (or 'Word', in St John's gospel) penetrated, enacting the beginning of an alchemical process which refined this base matter into Creation. As a result of heat and light, we have an ethereal substance that Vaughan calls the *Anima*, which is like Lull's *argent vive*. It is feminine, too, and is the word for 'soul' as well as for 'breath'. Out of this *Anima* come all the other levels of being – reaching down to the elemental level and the physical level here.

The hermetic view of the elements was mystical, too. Air was seen as a magical element, full of imagination and spirits, while water was the link between air and earth, as well as 'above' and 'below'. Earth was the ground of Creation, like a womb or matrix in which all generation takes place, receiving all the cosmic influences from the stars.

Try for a moment taking each element and picturing it to yourself in this way. Remember that each element is seen here as spiritual and as having an invisible as well as a visible function.

So matter here is both body and spirit – and the two blend into each other. And the Stone? These alchemists saw it as material light, or 'embodied light', for which Christ was the prototype. Christ was the perfect man; the Stone, perfect matter, matter realized through consciousness, through which we have purification, awakening and redemption ...

But if all this seems too abstract, here is a poem by George Herbert, written at this time, that speaks of this purity as a prayer and a realization:

The Elixir

Teach me, my God and King,
In all things thee to see,
And what I do in anything
To do it as for thee.

A man that looks on glass,
On it may stay his eye;
Or if he pleaseth, through it pass,
And then the heaven espy.

All may of thee partake;
Nothing shall so be mean,

Which with this tincture 'for thy sake'
Will not grow bright and clean.

A servant with this clause
Makes drudgery divine;
Who sweeps a room, as for thy laws,
Makes that and the action fine.

This is the famous stone
That turneth all to gold;
For that which God doth touch and own
Cannot for less be told.

It is as pure a statement of alchemy as we could still find – at a
time when the seeds of decline had already been sown.

THE ECLIPSE BY SCIENCE

Nobody seriously doubted the actual possibility of transmutation until this time, such was the strength of what alchemy
promised and its effect on people, whether conscious or not. But
by the seventeenth century we hear the first dissenting voices,
like Semler, in Germany, who openly said that the Elixir was impossible after he'd been duped by yet another quack, Baron
Hirschen. And if the number of pseudo-alchemists around was-
n't already enough evidence, the increasing research into actual
chemical changes hammered nails into an ever-expanding coffin.
Theory and generalization became practice and detailed experiment, the Royal Society was founded in London and Robert
Boyle's *The Sceptical Chymist* set the new tone.

It is vital to realize, though, that the aims of alchemy and
chemistry were in fact completely different, and that they are
different traditions as well. Chemistry's roots lie in pharmacy,
in Paracelsus' emphasis on experiment and medicine, and in
Descartes' mechanical view of matter,[16] which led to taking
things apart rather than seeing them whole. If alchemy is like a

stained-glass window, then chemistry is the analysis of its fragments, taken away from the one light shining through them. And as matter began to be seen as separate from mind, so it began to be seen as mechanical – obeying laws that could be fixed and proven.

So, the aim of chemistry was not the perfection of matter, but its analysis. This is what we see with Robert Boyle (d.1691) in his experiments with the boiling point of liquids, freezing water, and combustion, and John Mayow (d.1679) with his near-discovery of oxygen before Priestley and Lavoisier. Booerhave, who was Professor of Chemistry at Leyden in Germany in the 1720s and 30s, went on with his *Elementa chemiae* to disprove what he saw as the errors of the alchemists.

It is a complex picture though – not least because of the latest 'mystical' discoveries of the New Physics. From where we are now it has become fashionable, for instance, to criticize Isaac Newton, famous for his discovery of the law of gravity, as a materialist and 'Newtonian' has become a dirty word. But actually Newton was steeped in alchemy in a way that profoundly influenced his vision until the end of his life, seeing – as Maynard Keynes put it – 'the whole universe and all that is in it as a riddle'. How else could he have finally described himself as being like a child playing on the shores of eternity? Significantly, perhaps, his writings on alchemy were lost. Science took a different direction. So did alchemy. And the direction that alchemy took brings us closer to the more recent admission by scientists that observer and observed cannot, after all, be separated. We are *in* the picture, whether we like it or not, and reality cannot simply be measured or controlled.

Alchemy laid the foundation for chemical science and as a result of it, laboratory apparatus was developed and a whole range of compounds were discovered, including sulphur, nitric acid (Geber), mercuric oxide, calomel, potassium sulphate, hydrochloric acid

(Valentinus). There was also the preparation of alcohol and Paracelsus' introduction of chemical substances into medicine. Alchemy deepened our awareness of matter in every way. What we can say, I think, is that the chemical process within it was a stumbling quest for something that can finally only be achieved spiritually. And who knows what our relationship to matter could be then?

ESOTERIC

It was in the nineteenth century that the metaphorical or mystical, inward significance of alchemy really began to emerge, although, as we've seen, the mystical element was present from the earliest times.

The nineteenth-century alchemical revival pointed increasingly inward to emphasize that 'Man himself is the vessel': we ourselves are the source of the *prima materia* and the mercury – and we are the flask and the containment for the process. So the flask (or athanor) becomes our bodies rather than an externalized piece of apparatus. Hence 'esoteric' here, meaning 'inward' (or 'for the initiated') with the specific connotation of needing to get *in* by understanding the literal *as* the metaphorical. So *we* become the vessel and the fire that heats it, as the process begins and develops – and we are the process. It is in us.

We could say that this is what the chemical process alone had missed: *that alchemists were seeking in matter what they first had to find in themselves.*

The most remarkable exposition of this came through a woman called Mrs Atwood (formerly Miss South) who is the basis for Lindsay Clarke's compelling character Louisa in *The Chymical Wedding*. With her father, Thomas South, she wrote *A Suggestive Enquiry into the Hermetic Mystery*, first published in 1850 and almost as immediately withdrawn. Her father was concerned that it gave away too much. He may also have been jealous of his daughter's achievement. Fortunately for us, not every copy was destroyed.[17]

In this work, and through its archaic style of expression, something very clear and inspired emerges. As well as arguing that we are the vessel, Mrs Atwood suggests that the 'first matter' – the material we work from – is in the realm of our imagination. It is literally our astral body (as Paracelsus argued) that needs purification in order to raise it to the level of the heart and the Divine. The 'manual' process through which this takes place is related to hypnosis (then recently discovered). While that can be seen to be limited, it does open up the whole area of how we gain access in a sustained way to our imaginations so the process can take place, which is really what Mrs Atwood is talking about. The main part of this present book is also an attempt to explore exactly that question.

At the same time, however, we have to take care to stay in touch with the physical. For, if alchemy is a mystical or inward process, it is also – as its history abundantly illustrates – a *physical* mysticism. This is its unique quality, and we need to remain aware of that, otherwise we leave the ground.

By the twentieth century, three strands in alchemy come forward like branches in a river, with a fourth that this book also represents. Traditional or literal alchemy continued, along with its quacks like the American Edward Pinter and more infamously Franz Tausend,[18] as well as its genuine adherents like Abdul-Muhyi, an Arab who visited England; Archibald Cockren, who wrote *Alchemy Rediscovered and Restored* in 1940 and who – as a trained scientist – claimed to have completed the process as he understood it; and Armand Barbault in France, whose *Gold of a Thousand Mornings* (1934) describes how he worked with organic matter, distilling 'vegetable gold' as a universal panacea. Both Cockren and Barbault, whose aim was to contribute to medicine, are in line with Paracelsus and they keep the door open for others who have followed.[19]

A second branch follows on from mystical alchemy, with the founding of the Order of the Golden Dawn, contemporary with the College of Psychic Studies, in London in 1887. Stories about the Golden Dawn are legion. Its membership included Mac-Gregor Mathers as well as the 'Great Beast' Aleister Crowley and the Irish Laureate W. B. Yeats, but aside from its instability on a level of personality, its serious aim was to create a structure for esoteric learning, with a series of grades the novice would work through. These included the Cabbala, the Tarot and astrology as well as various rituals that are close to Freemasonry. With alchemy, the emphasis was on its symbolism, adapted into ritual and imaginative work, alongside the use of alchemical language. The path of knowledge *itself* became known as 'the Great Work' or 'the Work'. There is no doubt that the Golden Dawn helped preserve alchemy as a major point of reference, as well as bringing alchemical language more into common awareness. Many books about esoteric subjects have drawn on the material it systematized and made available.

Alchemy also surfaces in the work of G. I. Gurdjieff (d.1949) who emphasized its inner nature in terms of internal awakening and transformation, linking the spirit and the body directly as part of one system, and understanding the natural functions of the body in this way. He is quoted by his friend, co-worker and scribe P. D. Ouspensky:

> But all this alchemy is inside us, not outside ... In man's inner alchemy higher substances are distilled out of other, coarser material which otherwise would remain in a coarse state.[20]

And with the third branch, we need to look more closely at the water ...

It was C. G. Jung who revived alchemy in a special way by bringing it into the psychological realm. He made it the foundation of
his archetypal psychology, where it has been fostered ever since
by those who have followed him, including Marie Louise von
Franz and most recently James Hillman. With Jung we find the
psychologist-as-alchemist, enriching and extending our understanding of the art.

Jung first noticed the relationship between the kinds of images
we see in alchemical pictures and the images in the dreams of
the patients or clients he was working with. These coincided
often with times of crisis or change and took place even though
the people concerned apparently had no knowledge of the subject. This prompted a long exploration on Jung's part, from 1920
onwards, which took him back to reading and trying to decipher
original texts he collected.

In his autobiography, *Memories, Dreams, Reflections*, he tells
us of a dream he had himself:

*Before I discovered alchemy, I had a series of dreams which
repeatedly dealt with the same theme. Beside my house stood
another, that is to say, another wing or annex, which was
strange to me. Each time I would wonder in my dream why I
did not know this house, although it had apparently always
been there. Finally came a dream in which I reached the other
wing. I discovered there a wonderful library, dating largely
from the sixteenth and seventeenth centuries. Large, fat folio
volumes, bound in pigskin, stood along the walls. Among
them were a number of books, embellished with copper engravings of a strange character, and illustrations containing
curious symbols such as I had never seen before. At the time I
did not know to what they referred; only much later did I recognize them as alchemical symbols. In the dream I was conscious only of the fascination exerted by them and by the
entire library.*[21]

The product of this fascination was his monumental study *Psychology and Alchemy* (1944). His argument is that alchemy is not fundamentally a process to do with chemistry, but to do with the psyche – literally, the imagination of our souls and our soul-being as physical beings. Jung believed alchemists were projecting or seeing their own unconscious. This meant, as far as he was concerned, that their own process as individuals was inextricably linked to the process they were working with – an insight that is of vital importance to us and which in a sense 'proves' what Mrs Atwood had intuited. So, as a result, Jung says:

> *The alchemical* opus *deals in the main not just with chemical experiments as such, but with something resembling psychic processes expressed in pseudochemical language.*[22]

This leads him to conclude with this:

> *I am therefore inclined to assume that the real root of alchemy is to be sought less in philosophical doctrines than in the projections of individual investigators. I mean by this that while working on his chemical experiments the operator had certain psychic experiences which appeared to him as the particular behaviour of the chemical process. Since it was a question of projection, he was naturally unconscious of the fact that the experience had nothing to do with matter itself (that is, with matter as we know it today). He experienced his projection as a property of matter; but what he was in reality experiencing was his own unconscious.*[23]

And some pages further on he adds:

> *It should now be sufficiently clear that from its earliest days alchemy had a double face: on the one hand the practical chemical work in the laboratory, on the other a psychological process, in part consciously psychic, in part unconsciously projected and seen in the various transformations of matter.*[24]

Jung has been criticized, by F. Sherwood-Taylor and Titus Burck-hardt, for not grounding his enquiry enough in actual history and in an awareness of the process as being *also* a chemical one. There is truth in this, but what Jung achieves, unlike the histori-ans, is an experience of alchemy *from the inside*. The circum-stances of his life made this not only possible but unavoidable – his seven-year breakdown, his relationship with his *soror mysti-ca*, Toni Wolf, who took him into the depths of his own psyche, and to his grasp of the 'collective unconscious' of humanity, gave him a unique and realized view. As a result his idea that alchemy prompts an experience of 'individuation' in our psyches – a jour-ney towards wholeness from their roots – is thoroughly alchemi-cal and in tune with what alchemy has always been striving for. The gift of his work helps this to be possible for us now. If he doesn't go further into how matter itself can be transmuted as a result, he goes far enough: as far as we have come. Full circle.

And where now? In our new recognition of our continuity with matter and energy we have come to another threshold. Alchemy is embedded in the attempts of alternative medicine,[25] in the deeper interpretations of astrology,[26] and increasingly in the awareness of artists who are realizing the power and sacred po-tential of their work to serve as an initiation beyond a merely aesthetic or literary level of existence. Jacques Bergier, whom I quoted at the beginning of this chapter, states the nature of this threshold most clearly in *The Morning of the Magicians*, in quot-ing his 'stranger', almost certainly Fulcanelli:[27]

> *All the same, I can tell you this much: you are aware that in the official science of today the role of the observer becomes more and more important. Relativity, the principle of indeter-minacy, show the extent to which the observer today inter-venes in all these phenomena. The secret of alchemy is this: there is a way of manipulating matter and energy so as to*

produce what modern scientists call 'a field of force'. This field acts on the observer and puts him in a privileged position vis-à-vis the Universe. From this position he has access to the realities which are ordinarily hidden from us by time and space, matter and energy. This is what we call 'the Great Work'.[28]

And in that, we may be able to open to a deeper realization, which is that alchemy is not only a process we seek out, but also one *that seeks out us* in the deepest current and experience of our lives. It is this I want to turn to now as we begin to prepare to go into the process itself.

You may find it useful to return to this chapter to refresh your memory or awareness and place in context some of what we are about to enter into, but essentially now I suggest that you leave aside all the strands and complexities of the story of alchemy and turn to an awareness of yourself and your own story. As a way of doing this, another brief meditation exercise follows.

Let go of these words now and take a moment to let your mind begin to be still. Just connect to the feeling of coming back to yourself.

Breathe, and allow your breath to deepen, and as you breathe, be aware of your breath going down, down, into your body, down from your mind.

And as you breathe down, as you allow your breath to go down, be aware of emptying – and then see if you can go to the place where you are emptying.

What does it feel like there? What is the energy like in your body?

Be aware that this is your receptive place. Then see if you can allow an image or picture to come forward from it.

See what it is trying to show you. Can you see what it needs from you? (Remember you can ask it, 'What do you need from me?')

Then, when you're ready, come back and make a drawing of your image, along with any notes you want to about what has been taking place here.

We want to be creative, but to be creative we first of all have to be receptive – to understand our receptivity and what separates us from it.

How receptive do you allow yourself to be? How could you be more so?

I would invite you to consider that, before we turn to the preparation for the work.

THREE

PREPARATION

V.I.T.R.I.O.L.: Visita interiora terrae; rectificando invenies occultem lapidem *(Visit the interior of the earth; through purification you will find the hidden stone).*

VALENTINUS

All inner work begins with work upon the shadow. It is the foundation of any psychological or spiritual path.

LLEWELYN VAUGHAN-LEE

PREPARATION

A flask in the shadow, inside the inner contours of your skin.

Preparation for the process itself is about earth and fire. It concerns two aspects; the 'first matter' (or *prima materia*,) that relates to earth and the 'first agent' that is another name for the fire. It both cases, preparation takes us deeper into ourselves – into a depth of earth that is also the body as a container or vessel and 'into the fire', as we say, that is also the concentration of our inward self.

So the first steps are *down* and *in*, and they involve three processes which we'll look at in turn. But first a word or two about timing. When do we begin? Alchemists say that the best time to begin the process is in the spring – especially in Aries (March and April), but also through Taurus and Gemini: signs that include fire, earth and the mind (air). If you are familiar at all with astrology, you might like to consult an astrological practitioner to see what is uppermost for you in your chart at this time – especially with reference to any transits you may be experiencing, as well as major aspects which are always going to be there and which will always be more or less active.

So let's take the first step.

Preparation begins with a quest for the *prima materia*, literally the material which is to be transformed, and alchemists have pictured this as a journey to a mine – a place that is under the surface and is dark.

This is where the first matter is to be found.

What can we say about it? *Prima materia* lies very deep. It is the most physical and mysterious thing there is. In itself it is deeper than concepts, words or ideas. It has been given many names (among which are 'sea', 'seed of things' and 'basic moistness')[1] and we cannot precisely define it – but it clearly exists on two levels.

At the deepest and purest level it is the original ground, the original state – a state deeper than chaos, that has been referred to as 'the Mother of all created things'. It is in the handful of black earth that Adam was said to have brought out of Paradise. So it is the first of all things, its substance (for alchemists) is Divine, and it is extremely fertile. Eximindus describes it as 'a certain primary everlasting and infinite nature which cooks and rules everything'.[2]

It has also been called *radix ipsius* (root of itself), dependent on nothing and no one. Like deep space, it is mirrored below, under the ground – and it has also been related to silver, or the feminine, and pictured as a pure spring that is the origin of Mercurius and the mercurial energy that is vital to the process at every stage.

Yet again it is called 'the hidden stone' – the stone that through the process becomes the Philosopher's Stone, transmuted and transforming.

Closer to our own frame of reference, we can call *prima materia* 'the ground of the soul'. It is out of this that our individual experience of it can come at a level that is closer to the surface and to us.

Prima materia in itself is passive, not active. Like a mirror, it is pure receptivity. In us, however, it is not so pure, and this is what is referred to in the journey to the mine, the journey 'to take possession of the raw subject'.[3]

The raw subject is the raw material in us, and it is this – our own hidden stone – that is the matter we need to take hold of, the 'matter in hand'. We can think of it as the unconscious that our conscious minds need to descend to, in order to feel and experience rather than think and control. Its impurities are our 'stuff', as we say, the trace elements of the psyche – knots, complexes, resistances, blockages – all a result of what we have lived and suffered. And it begins to weigh, to get heavy, we can see it is our lead, our heavy metal. As a result, it often feels depressing, both emotionally and physically.

And yet we need it. And we need to find it – or perhaps let it find us.

Try the following exercise.

Sitting quietly again for a moment or two, just see if you can reflect on what drew you or guided you to this book. Where were you at the time? What was happening to you and around you?

What was your feeling in relationship to it? See if you can reconnect to it, and follow it from your mind towards your body, closing your eyes.

Follow the feeling down and see where it wants to go. See if you can trust it. Where is it taking you?

Or, if you're stuck, where does it want to take you? Remember, you can ask it.

Where are you finding yourself? Look at the ground under your feet. See if you can see – or feel – where you are.

What is there in front of you? Take a moment to see what it is and then see if you can take it, or some of it, into your hands.

And then begin your journey back up to the daylight and when you're ready, open your eyes and make a note of what you've found.

And that brings us to the second part of the preparation.

Initiations of any kind are usually preceded by some kind of purification or cleansing and here 'the subject' is us: you and I. The aim is that the subject is 'rid of its attle ...' or dross – or, as we might say, our shit. This is not so much the stuff we work with as the stuff that gets in the way, that works *against* us and prevents real change. It is related to ego and to the mask we wear as well as, more practically, to a lack of strength or will and an inability to sustain concentration, so that we stay distracted on the surface of things.

The entire process is demanding at any moment and it requires our strength. There is no avoiding this, as every alchemist knows. However, the more we give to it, the more it gives to us.

And, as many alchemists have stated, the process can only be accomplished with God's help and completed with God: in other words, through what is higher than ourselves. So we need to offer up a prayer. As the *Mappae Clavicula*, a twelfth-century English text, has it:

> *Prayer you are to recite during the operation or the fusion that follows, in order that the gold may be formed.*[4]

This doesn't have to be a standard prayer: it can be our own. It is the state of mind that prayer brings that is important here, as a gesture of opening – and not only in our minds but in our hearts as well.

Pause for a moment and reflect on your experience of prayer. Can you see what your prayer might be here?

Can you feel where that would connect you? Where this would bring you to in yourself?

Take a few minutes with this. You may also like to write down what comes to you here, whether or not your experience comes in the form of words.

The power of prayer lies in its ability to soften and attune us, so it is again related to receptivity. The second aspect of purification follows on from this and is a more active expression. It is simply commitment – commitment that follows a choice to actually do something. Obviously, here it's not just a casual choice, like going for a drink or a walk; it is something more. It is a choice we have to make for ourselves. There is one consolation, though. The size of the choice we make always relates to the size of the purpose involved and choosing always releases energy. We choose, then the thing begins to move, quicken and flow.

So commitment here is about the energy in the experience of saying YES, the energy when a path, like an avenue opens.

Think of saying 'Yes.'
What is your relationship to saying so?
And what is the effect for you when you do?

Commitment here is also about recognizing the qualities we need to stay with the process once it has begun. Alchemists have emphasized these in terms of forbearance and patience, recognizing, as we shall, that we are tempered within the process itself, as part of the journey. We shall need all our resources as well as our humour on the journey – and we shall need to side-step self-pity, too.

But most of all what we need is to be 'one-pointed': we need to keep our concentration. The process in an inner space it can be all too easy to take for granted. 'Oh yes, it's going fine,' we say – and then we blow it. We come out of it, seduced by something incidental that passes as quickly as the distraction it creates, leaving us trying to get back into it again. As Thomas Norton affirmed, no doubt from experience:

The mind must be in harmony with the work, and the work must be above all else.[5]

We are preparing a flask, the container that is ourselves. We touch on it every time we come into stillness and the recognition of what need to stay in and with ourselves. We recognize it every time we experience needing space – needing to be on our own for a moment, or even for days. The sides of the flask are weak at first, like the thin meniscus of a soap bubble. We need to strengthen and solidify them, and this is where the third of the three processes I mentioned comes in to help us.

THE PREPARATION OF THE SECRET FIRE

The Secret Fire, as well as being refered to as the 'first agent' – which we can understand as the first active factor, the first element necessary for the process to happen – is also called the *Ignis Innaturalis*; in other words, it is not simply fire as we would literally think of it. It is described as:

Dry water that does not wet the hands,
a fire burning without flames ...

It is a hidden fire, an inner heat. It is the invisible energy that sustains matter – and in us it is the energy or fire we build up in ourselves by being contained, by not leaking it out.

So it is an 'unnatural fire', and the discipline it requires doesn't come easily. Its nature is of a different kind and it recalls another key alchemical saying: 'Nature can overcome nature.'

Like a taste, the secret fire has to be acquired. It has to be prepared, it has to be created – and its secret is in the act of will we make every time we decide, for instance, to work. The nature we overcome is whatever prevents us from doing that.

As as result of this, the fire that brings us *in* to ourselves is a fire of meditation and contemplation, literally a 'dry water' and 'a fire burning without flames'. We can also think of it as the heat that comes through a healer's hands. So it is an energy in the body as well as a state of mind. Meditation and contemplation are the active ingredients here: they bring us to a more central part of ourselves and allow a deeper energy to come into being. This, then, is the fire.

> *Take a moment to connect to the feeling of fire, or fieriness,*
> *in you.*
> *Where do you feel it in your body?*
> *Then see it. What does it look like?*
> *How do you feel towards it?*
> *What do you need to allow it more? Ask it.*

Meditation and contemplation – an active opening up, mulling over and reflecting – are vital to any creative work, including this. We can't really enter into the alchemical process without them – and in themselves they assist us every step of the way. They help us towards where we need to go now, which is into the flask itself: what alchemists call 'the closed body of the house'. They help us to be still, to centre and to concentrate, and they help us to regain our balance when we lose it, clearing us of everything we take in from the outside, quietening and recharging us within. They give us back a sense of the shape and weight of ourselves, of our edges and the boundaries of our skin.

So let's go inside now, and take another step in.

Take a moment or two to relax. Sit and feel your breathing.

Feel your feet on the ground and your body on the chair or floor where you are sitting. Close your eyes.

And then again, breathe down, allowing your breath to deepen, into your body, while bringing your awareness of the flask to mind.

How do you begin to feel this flask in yourself? Where are you feeling it in your body?

What does it look like? How does it image itself to you?

What is it made of? What is its quality, texture and colour?

Can you see what your flask is trying to show you?

If you are having any difficulty with it, ask it what it needs from you.

Are you in it or outside it? How could you get into it?

What happens when you do? Stay with it.

Be aware of what it is like in there and of how you are feeling. What connection does the space inside the flask need from you?

Then, slowly, with your eyes still closed, make a movement in-side yourself to the edges of your skin: to your belly, to your arms, your thighs, your feet, your chest, your throat and your head ... really feeling the space inside your body.

Now, why not make a drawing of your flask, so as to anchor it, along with any notes from the experience – or as a result of it.

And then *Deo volente,* as they say. God willing.

May the Work begin.

FOUR

THE LESSER WORK

NIGREDO

There is in our chemistry a certain noble substance, in the beginning thereof is wretchedness with vinegar, but in its ending joy with gladness. Therefore I have supposed that the same will happen to me, namely that I shall suffer great difficulty, grief, weariness at first, but in the end shall come to glimpse pleasanter and easier things.

MICHAEL MAIER

Yes, my eyes are closed to your light. I am an animal, a nigger. But I can be saved.

ARTHUR RIMBAUD, SEASON IN HELL

The ground of the soul is dark.

JAMES HILLMAN

NIGREDO

Wisp already winter mist at the height of summer
The ravens circling around the barren fallow field.

'In the midst of life, there is death.'

Alchemy, as its etymology suggests, begins in darkness. We have had a first sight of it already with the *prima materia* – and now it goes further, much further in and down into the night, a Dark Night. So the black fecund earth of *prima materia*, also referred to as antimony and described as *nigrum nigrius nigro* ('a black blacker than black'), is taken forward here into a full-scale descent of the mind. This is the first stage of the Lesser Work: *nigredo*. This descent, this dying, points inward into the body – inward and back into the physical ground of our being. Alchemists have a saying: 'No generation without corruption.'

Or we could say no birth, or rebirth, without death. Death first.

The essence of *nigredo* is a blackening and a putrefying, which is why it is also referred to as *calcinatio* (*calcine*: 'to burn') and *mortificatio* (literally, 'to mortify'). It concerns primarily the death of the Old King or ego which he symbolizes (*see p.32*) and it takes place under Saturn, which, you will remember, for earlier alchemists was the furthest planet from the sun. Saturn as a planet is associated with lead – the *nigredo* is the lead. Saturn is also associated with the intellect or mind, as well as with form and structure.

So we are entering into a death of the mind in a place that is farthest from the sun – far from light and seemingly from hope, as the provocative illustration of the king suggests. Here the king, who in legend is called King Gold, is surrounded by a gang of alchemists in monks' cowls with their clubs raised, poised to strike.

Other alchemical images of *nigredo* include the *caput mortuum*[1] (or 'dead head'); the green lion, who is the subversive, instinctual force of Nature, swallowing the sun of the ego; ravens, who are death-birds, picking over a desert of human skeletons; and coffins and sarcophagi – and the smell is of decomposition and rotting, of something gone badly off, which also has to do with what is literally happening in the flask. The main single image is of the *sol niger* – a black sun shining over a lifeless land. We can understand this as the sun's descent and the descent of the light in us that is also consciousness.

So consciousness descends towards the unconscious – towards what we cannot see (it is black) and cannot, in our heads, control. Even the king seems unaware of what is about to descend on him (*see figure*).

Physically, at this first stage the first matter and the first agent are put 'in a mortar made of agate'. The *prima materia* is pulverized and rolled like dough, mixed with the first agent and 'moistened with dew'.

Remember to take this metaphorically as well as literally as you see it in your mind's eye.

The 'compost' is then enclosed in a sealed vessel (that is the flask) or 'philosophic egg'. This philosophic egg refers to consciousness, or awareness, and birth. The egg is a symbol of all of these.

Inside the flask, this egg is kept at a constant temperature for long periods – blood-warm as a hen sitting on her eggs; body-warm, they say, as fresh horse dung. Later on, things get much hotter; for now, here at the beginning, the fire heating the flask and the inner fire inside it need to be restrained from overheating 'or the work will be lost'. In other words, the clay or glass will shatter. (No doubt, this happened many times and the process had to be begun all over again.)

So the flask, the fire and its contents are in place.

Meanwhile, in our story, something of particular importance has taken place and this brings us to Sol and Luna.

Boy meets girl, man meets woman, brother meets sister (or the other way round) – and potential queen meets potential king. Their meeting is a key thread in the overall process – and their story is about the realization of love.

But theirs is no ordinary or orthodox kind of loving. For a start, it exists on two levels: outwardly in terms of the relationship between the alchemist and his *soror mystica*, as companion and assistant, or as the male brother equivalent for a woman; inwardly in relationship to Sol and Luna, representing the masculine and feminine respectively as inner archetypes – and more literally as sulphur and quicksilver.

The *soror mystica* may exist outwardly in the form of another person or inwardly as a part of oneself. Her first gesture is one of silence, raising her finger to her lips. As well as being a gesture of secrecy it is also an invitation *not to speak but to feel* and this remains true at every stage. The gesture relates to the containment that the process requires, which means staying inside the flask.

She – or he – is not exactly a wife or husband or lover, although she could be any of these. She exists at another level. We need to look more closely at what she is called so as to enter into an understanding of how Sol and Luna relate from when they meet. *Soror mystica:* the clue is in the name, meaning 'mystical sister or brother'. Whether this sister or brother exists outwardly or inwardly, the relationship is unusual and unusually charged, and it brings us into an area that is still taboo because it is incestuous. It may not be literally so, but it feels like it and this is what is important. The *soror mystica* is someone uncannily familiar – even perhaps a part of oneself. That is the feeling we need to connect to here.

Sol and Luna meet, then, and the inevitable happens – they make love, as in alchemical terms, they must. They often appear crowned, making love in water (*see figure*). As the *Rosarium* puts it:

Make one water out of two waters. If you have understood my short indication, the whole course of action will be under your feet.[2]

And as a similar text adds:

Sun and moon must have intercourse like that of man and woman, otherwise the object of our art cannot be obtained. All other teaching is false and erroneous.[3]

This is a composite meeting, where every part of both is involved. It is man and woman, it is brother and sister, it is mother

CONIVNCTIO SIVE
Coitus.

and son, and it is father and daughter. In alchemical terms, it is *coniunctio*, that literally means 'a joining of the opposites'. It is sex and it is entry, which is why it is also referred to as *coitus* as well as 'the opening of the matrix' in either a woman or a man. It is uninhibited and it is lusty. It happens the way it happens and it is not neat and tidy. Its function is to *open the body*, the way penetration does. And it gives us body, if nothing else. Alchemists sometimes refer to it as the 'Gross Work' as well, coming just before the 'Lesser Work' we are now in. And however we understand or experience *coitus* at this stage, the point is that it is undifferentiated. It is as yet unconscious, as any marriage can be: it is unpurified, if you like, unworked for.

And its outcome is not what we think it might be, although it corresponds exactly to the beginning of a relationship in terms of its vision and potential. In it, we catch a glimpse of what *could be* – and, at another level, *is*. Out of their love-making, which confronts deep pain and regressive trauma, returning to childhood and the deepest levels of primal being, comes a vision of the androgyne or hermaphrodite that is simultaneously man and woman, woman and man, the opposites blended inwardly. And out of the pregnancy of the situation we see the youthful Mercurius emerging, a new kind of being who is both innocent and experienced, free and whole. Often portrayed with wings, holding a staff of healing two snakes are coiled round, his body is masculine and his soul is feminine. We could perhaps imagine him with a feminine body and a masculine soul as well.

He has been described as the incarnate or secret side of God, or the Divine, embracing light and shadow, moving between both, youthful and fresh. He is always the third point or third thing in relationship to Sol and Luna, both as their guiding influence – like Lady Alchymia herself – and their product or child. He holds the key to their androgynous being. Throughout the process, he is the principle of analogy that connects one thing to another (stone to tincture, to Red King and White Queen).

To return to Sol and Luna, they meet and make love, and then an extraordinary thing happens. They tread the golden field together and then it all begins to fall dark. Gold to black.

We come back to the flask, with Sol and Luna inside it: inside the philosophic egg as masculine and feminine, sulphur and quicksilver. Here they begin to react and fight as the *nigredo* itself begins. As Flamel imagines it:

> After both have been placed in the 'vessel' of the grave, they begin to bite one another savagely, and, on account of their great poison and raging fury, do not let go of each other – unless the cold should deter them – until both, as a result of their dripping poison and deadly wounding, are drenched in blood, so that they finally kill one another and drown in their own poison, which, after their death, will transmute them into living and perpetual water, after they have lost, with their downfall and decomposition, their first, natural forms, in order to acquire a single, new, nobler and better form ...[4]

So what we have now is the reverse of the *coniunctio* that is perhaps nevertheless implicit in it as the shadow side erupts. Sol and Luna are now completely at odds: polarized, absolutely unable to see one another. A savage inversion has taken place so that everything that is erotic between them points towards death and at the same time everything that has to do with death is aimed, consciously or not, towards birth. In the mad heat of the moment and in all their raw emotion, they don't see this. They are black fire. Sometimes they are pictured as lion and lionness locked together, clawing at each other; and again sometimes they are charging full-tilt at each other in a joust, lances raised, Sol on a dragon and Luna on a griffin.

These are also violent images for the base metal – the lead – that is being broken down, bubbling and spitting as a result of acidic activity as the *materia* is divested of its original form.

As Sol and Luna rage, revealing their impurity, they are purified. The same argument holds true for the base metal in us.

It has to be broken down before it can be transmuted – its original form has to be destroyed.

So, as the blackness increases, this is what is taking place. Some alchemists have described it as a dark impenetrable cloud that begins to fill the flask like shaken-up sediment or dust.

Finally, Sol and Luna 'die', and their death, like a post-coital sinking, leads to separation and a long process of decay as the blackness thickens and weighs, slowing ... until everything in the flask is putrefied, rotting and stinking, until there is a dissolving, deeper than form or image or even thought of any kind, that is the liquid *nigredo*, the *nigrum nigrius nigro*:

> *This darkness darker than darkness,*
> *This black of blacks.*

as they say.

We are at a primal level now. We are in the black unknown. We are at a level of formless origin, in a darkness that only dying knows. The sun is in total eclipse. Our minds have gone.

In real time, this blackness, though we can glimpse it in seconds, lasts for months at least – maybe even longer.

Finally, a change long past hoping comes as they say 'when a starry aspect appears on the surface'. Then there is a drying out, an evaporation after the boiling that creates a 'metallic volatile humidity', leaving a residue of precious *ash* – out of which now the Mercury of the Wise appears. So we have Mercurius again, but this time at the depth; and not out of the union of opposites, but their destruction. It is a very different kind of birth, like the calm after a storm, brought forth from a long night of depression, breakdown and despair, as well as the disassociation that Sol and Luna enact before they separate.

See if you can get a feeling for this ash now, in silence, for a moment or two. How do you feel it? What is its quality?

So, in *nigredo*, we have a strong movement from solid (the base metal) to liquid (the liquid blackness) to ash (the residue). The point of it all, as Burckhardt puts it, is to 'free the soul from its coagulation and paralysis' – in other words, to free the soul from the grip of the ego and the intellectual mind. Here, in the house of Saturn, who is very precise, the soul's form is burnt and melted down, so, as he says, 'it reverts to its original unconditioned state': in other words, to a level before conditioning – that moulding of our personalities that we have all experienced. So with the ash, what we have left *is the soul*.

At this point, I would like to suggest an exercise so you can open to the experience of *nigredo* for yourself. You may want to do this exercise in a darkened room.

Sitting comfortably, just give yourself a minute or two to let go of all you've read so far. When you have a feeling of just being in yourself, close your eyes.

Begin to move from your mind back down into your flask. You may imagine this as the sun or light going down from your head, darkening as it descends, or you may already be in darkness.

Be aware of the quality and feeling of the darkness. Be aware of how your heart is feeling. And be aware of your body. What is the sensation?

Now see if you can connect to a time when a darkness came into your life – when you experienced something dying, breaking down or decaying. It may be some time ago or it may be happening right now.

Where were you? Or are you? What was happening to you and around you?

See if you can re-enter the picture and let the memories find you again.

How do you feel it in your body? How do you feel it in your heart? And how do you feel it in your mind? Take it slowly.

As you connect to this experience now, see if an image comes forward from it. Again, trust what wants to come.

Take a moment to really see your image, holding it in your mind's eye, and then reflect on what it might be saying to you or showing you about that time or about now.

Then, when you're ready, come back and draw your image, using whatever colours you need, to ground and give it substance. Write up any notes you want to make.

You might want to reflect further on your experience with this before reading on, or even find a friend or partner to share it with. Remember you are in the flask now. Be aware of what your needs are, particularly in and with your body. Whether you are alone or with another, I would suggest you take a break before continuing to read this chapter.

The *nigredo* is really a head-on, ego-shattering experience, especially when we experience it for the first time – and it can leave a real residue of fear about continuing with the Work. Every alchemist knows this fear and hesitation – and it has often been said that the beginning of the Work is the most difficult, and even dangerous. This is when most of the mistakes and lapses in concentration are likely to take place. *Nigredo* is a very powerful space. Jung expresses this, tellingly:

> *The dread and resistance which every natural human being experiences when it comes to delving too deeply into himself is, at bottom, the fear of the journey to Hades. If it were only resistance that he felt, it would not be so bad. In actual fact, however, the psychic substratum, that dark realm of the unknown, exerts a fascinating attraction that threatens to become the more overpowering the further he penetrates into it. The psychological danger that arises here is the disintegration of personality into its functional components, i.e. the separate functions of consciousness, the complexes, hereditary units, etc.[5]*

So our resistance is understandable. But at the same time, it is happening to us. We have little apparent choice in the matter. For most people I know who have had *nigredo* experience, there is the feeling that 'there is nothing you can do', and this accords exactly with the experience of Saturn. As hard as you may try to get out, it's as if there is a counterforce pushing and even squeezing you back *in*, as anyone who has experienced the astrological 'Saturn Return' (initially between 28 and 30)[6] knows. Saturn is a hard taskmaster, thorough and unremitting, and we have Pluto with all its connotations of raking the depths in here as well. While Saturn and Pluto are different, their work is connected. It is to *get the ego inside the flask*, and it is to separate out, or deconstruct, the many and different strands of ego personality.

In the beginning, we resist this. We don't want to know. We can reject the experience and that can often manifest as anger ('It's all a load of rubbish anyway'). Rejection or denial is usually followed by an experience of suffocation and of poison erupting, with melancholy, grief and bitterness – emotions that may surprise us with their strength. In the *Rosarium* there is a saying that in the *nigredo* 'the brain turns black'. We begin to see everything in a black light. It is as if the shadow part of ourselves becomes us – and we may think it mean and miserly. I say 'we may think' because the shadow can be positive, too, and it is important to remember this. *Nigredo* can act as a powerful corrective for those of us who think we are all light. The saying holds true: 'The stronger the light, the longer the shadow' – especially if we are unaware of it. This is also Pluto's realm.

These reactions are all to do with the Old King in us who of course wants to stay on his throne and rule. The personification of the ego here is masculine, but he could equally be an Old Queen, a proud, imperious grandmother. It is this part of us that has to go. Why? *Because it obstructs the soul.*

In the end the ego gives up, but usually unwillingly. Its strategies for self-protection are endless, and the process can be lengthy and repetitive. This is because we fear insecurity, naturally, we fear what we don't know. And we lack trust, always. 'So, alright, this is going to go – but then what?' And we can't say. At this stage, a real lowering or deepening into depression comes in that signifies the descent is actually taking place. We are weighed down with a sense of heaviness and grief that is the lead. There can be a sense of 'caving in' as well, and of a lack of physical strength and vitality. This experience, which brings us to the dross, is also keeping us *in*. And then – and this is an important moment – it's as if 'there is no way out, only in'. This is the beginning of acceptance.

So we go in – and this is where breakdown, or what feels like breakdown, can take place. The unconscious itself is simultaneously light and dark as the *prima materia* itself is: it contains riches, but it also contains dangers. It is not a comfortable place. It holds all we have suppressed, and actively suppress, in the name of sanity. The real danger is where there is no containment for what is going on, in which case there is no flask either. Then the process is projected outside us, for instance as murder, or even suicide. What has been called 'lead mania' is also a possibility here, which can go with the feeling of being poisoned as well as grey-faced. It is very likely, as Johannes Fabricius has suggested,[7] that alchemists in their laboratories suffered delusional states as a result of the toxic nature of the materials they were working with. However, inwardly we can see this positively as well as in terms of the imagination and also dreams. As Marie Louise von Franz puts it, referring to the kind of dreams that usually come up in *nigredo*:

It is just those dreams which are so valuable; they have an unapproachable, disgusting shell of depressing blackness but within that is the light of the unconscious. It is often in the depressing motifs of the dream that the light is to be found, and naturally it is also to be found in the shadowy impulses which are full of meaning if one can lovingly investigate them with an attitude that accepts the paradox. [8]

That is wise guidance here. You might like to consider the imagery that came up for you during the exercise in relationship to this as well.

Nigredo can often be about the death of illusion, too – the death of what is after all not real, or not *yet* real, as painful as this can be, especially in the context of a relationship. As one man shared during a session: 'We had to separate to begin to find a solution,' and then, seeing the significance of what he'd said, he smiled the ghost of a smile. This death of illusion is a lonely business, but like anything major in our lives, we often have to go through it alone to find the strength it can bring – just as we think it is tearing us apart. As Ruth White once said, in a phrase I have always remembered: 'The better the quality of the negative, the deeper the development.'

Nigredo may seem to sever us from all the light we've ever known, but it always brings us to something deeper in ourselves where that light can shine again – whether it is in our own body, as a result of being ungrounded, or in relationship to a man or a woman, or in connection to our own authority rather than someone else's, whether as an individual, a parent or an institution.

So *nigredo*, strangely, is not just about pain and darkness, though it can (bloody well) seem like it at the time. This is where acceptance is vital, so we can see, in a deeper way, the initiation it represents. We need above all here, I think, to see *what we are being brought down to* – the ash, the soul. Then we gain the soul's way of seeing and understanding.

So as you review your experience of *nigredo*, I want to suggest you ask yourself these questions: 'What for?', 'What was I (or am I) being brought down to?', remembering that your dreams can also be an invaluable source of information here – dreams you may have had or are having as a result of working with this.

☿

Collectively, we can see *nigredo* everywhere we look in our world at this time, more so than any other stage in the process. We are in a Global Nigredo. The Old King (or Queen) is hanging on in various guises – from politicians to military tyrants to gurus and institutions of all kinds who are revealing their *own* shadow and misuse of power.

Nigredo is most obvious in rampant capitalism, the lust for material gold that is creating an ever-widening gulf between rich and poor on our planet. The world as we know it is in crisis emotionally, ecologically and spiritually, and we can see the effects of mortification everywhere, and putrefaction, shockingly, in the faces and emaciated bodies of the homeless and the starving. As poet Norman Jope, an initiate of *nigredo*, puts it, there is 'a pox in Roseland' (*see his poem opposite*).[9]

The problem and vast potential tragedy with all of this is *that it is unconscious* – and depending on how we see or respond to it, it will either go on perpetuating itself like a machine or it will come through (as it must, if we are to survive) to another place. There are real signs that this 'coming through' is happening, but it cannot be taken for granted, and it involves – inevitably – each one of us, and at every level.

So alchemy's stance of individual change is compellingly relevant to us now – to all of us, for there are no 'chosen few' anymore.

So we have to have the courage to die in a different way, to ourselves and our emotional egos. We have to find the ash, to find another way through.

We have to come into *solutio*.

The Pox in Roseland

The poppies multiply as wasps get larger.
Wheatfields lose their boundaries. The houses ripen.
Free papers move across the seeded mudplots,
Dashing out what brains they have on polished fences
As the Datsuns, Vauxhalls, Fords, Toyotas, Ladas, Audis
Grind into the drives. Keys turn, to prise
A pinnied kiss, a six-cal mini-supper and a night of
Sit-coms. A freight train goosesteps over clayey
Sub-soils. The single village pub is filled with brags
Concerning dividends and food in baskets. The poppies
Wave. The wasps fake honeycombs. The bees
Have almost burst with pollen – are obese, asthmatic –
And they humble heavily. A circle swells
In ripening corn, a mile into the field,
That no-one sees. The shadow of the trolleys
On the local drive-in Sainsbury's read –
Mene, Mene ... And he tells her
It is over, that the figures will not balance
And that chaos theory slaughters economics.
Beyond their walls, the poppies drink
The stings of wasps, dream death in shocks of violet.

NORMAN JOPE

FIVE

THE LESSER WORK

SOLUTIO

Go to the woman who washes her sheets and do as she does.

ATALANTA FUGIENS

If you will not clean the impure body and make it white and give back to it its soul, you will have accomplished nothing in this magistery.

ROSARIUM PHILOSOPHORUM

What whiteness can you add to this whiteness,
What candour?

EZRA POUND, THE CANTOS (LXXX)

To make white the heart is an opus contra naturam. *We expect the heart to be red as its natural blood, green as its hopeful desire ...*

JAMES HILLMAN, THOUGHT OF THE HEART

SOLUTIO

The night sky's translucent skein – your raised face and eyes.
Pure smoke of lit cloud drifting across the moon...

Solutio in every way continues the work done in *nigredo* – in fact so much so that these two stages are really two sides of the same coin that we can imagine side by side just as the black and the white of the yin and yang symbol merge with and mirror each other:

In *solutio*, we come into the whiteness beyond the blackness: we pass from emotion into feeling, from the solar plexus towards the heart. Emotion and feeling are frequently confused – *solutio* clarifies the difference. Emotion belongs to everything we've seen in the *nigredo*, whereas feeling, always softer, more receptive, freer and clearer, is something quite different. It connects us to spirit. At the same time, emotion, rightly understood, is the fuel that feeling can come out of through purification and fire. So now, after the descent of the mind in *nigredo*, in *solutio* we are rising – we are going into the heart.

Solutio brings us to that core alchemical saying *solve et coagula*, dissolve and re-form, which we can understand here as purify and re-form, or re-unite.

The essence of *solutio* is a whitening, which is why it is also called *ablutio* (ablution, i.e. washing), *baptisma* (as in 'baptism', here with fire as well as water) and *albedo*, with its connotations of 'albino'. It has specifically to do with the soul, which is the deep part of us that is feeling, and spirit, which is the higher part that reaches beyond our minds. It is where Luna and the feminine principle come into their own as a transforming power.

Solutio is literally the softening or purifying of *the soul itself*, then, freed from the carapace of the ego as we've seen with *nigredo* – and as a stage it is associated with Jupiter first and then the moon. Jupiter is the antithesis of Saturn. Where Saturn is all about constriction, Jupiter relieves and releases us into expansion – like a breathing out. The moon, particularly the full moon, completes the stage as the silvery whiteness itself. An analogy for the experience of *solutio* is the progress through the lunar phases from dark to full. Also, just as we have an association between Saturn and Pluto in *nigredo*, so here we have Neptune, planet of the deep sea and dreaming. These are the astrological associations. So we are now one step closer to the sun, and we go by way of the moon. The moon comes first.

Images of *solutio* include the king at sea, drowning, calling out for help; or in a heat bath, like a sauna, sweating it out; the pelican (*see figure*), named after a particular retort in the laboratory with its two arms or wings like a jug – and here, piercing its own breast, symbolizing contact with the heart and the conscience of the heart.

Also we have more obvious images of purity: the unicorn, symbolizing the spirit with the strength of its horn, a beast which, it was said, could only be caught by a virgin; we have virgins, too, in relationship to Luna, as a quality of feminine purity, not as a denial of sexuality (remembering the word 'virgin' originally referred to a woman who was 'at one in herself'); also the lunar egg, symbolizing rebirth; and the *Rosa Alba* or White Rose, as the blossoming of spiritualized romantic love. Besides Sol and Luna themselves, the most significant image that underpins all of these is the aim of the *solutio* itself: the making of the white stone.

The white stone – as opposed to the black sun – is where light becomes solid as a result of repeated distillation and coagulation (*solve et coagula*). It is a pure spiritual substance and the end-point of the Lesser Work. For some alchemists it was the goal of the *whole* Work – we will see, however, why the rest went further.

So we have the ash at the end of the night; we have the black-ened dead body and the blackened mass inside the flask. The alchemist is stretched out on his bed in exhaustion and then out-side, in the dark, rain begins softly falling. Slowly the darkness begins to lighten and from inside it emerges a white dawn of clouds obscuring the sun ...

There is a rising. And inside the flask, with an initial cooling; 'this principle [the ash] flies through the alchemical air, in the microcosm of the egg, receiving the celestial and purifying influ-ences from above'.[1] So there is an upward movement, a freeing like breathing out. And then 'it falls again, sublimated, on the New Earth that must eventually emerge'.[2] This points ahead to the *coagulatio*, the next stage. What we see now is a repeated *washing*, congealing and redissolving of the matter inside the flask as the fire is slowly intensified. It is basically a process of heating and vaporizing which is equivalent to sublimation, which literally means to 'raise up'.

Sublimation is the key here. It is the whitening that the *Rosar-ium* refers to as 'the whiteness called air'; and in terms of the washing, the water involved here is 'the water of wisdom' seen as tears.

This is the process of purification and it is as thorough as it is intense, as the heat gets stronger. The matter is whitened through to the bone – and this refers to all the layers of the *corpus* or body. It continues, with repeated cleansing, until the whiteness begins to become strong and clear – until clarity dawns, in this strange lunar day that could also be night. This is the purifica-tion of the body that is the first part of *solutio* and what happens inside the flask.

The second part has to do with the spiritualization of the body which the white stone is also a metaphor for, in terms of ourselves. The heat is turned up again until from the repeated distillation and coagulation of the body (the material), appears a residue – *the stone*. And as the substance of the stone begins to emerge, a beautiful and unexpected thing happens: colours appear, colours that fan out and cover the whole spectrum, preceding the whiteness itself. This is called the *cauda pavonis* or peacock's tail; opening out, irridescent, it represents wholeness or a healing, an eruption of beauty in the psyche as well as the miraculous, for the spiritualization of the body is a miraculous thing.

The white stone itself is the whiteness or purity beyond all colours and effects. It is pulverized into form until all trace of the blackness is gone – so it is a physical reality, not just an idea, which is why some alchemists (Flamel and Valentinus included) see it as Christ.[3] The white stone involves a real heart opening, with all the pain that can entail, and out of that comes the White Rose, the bloom on the stone that is transcendent, realized and earned – that is love.

Once the whiteness is attained, the alchemist is said to have enough strength to resist the ardours of the fire. This means we have become strong enough to not get swept away and lose either the ground under our own feet or our centres. We have become strong enough to hold spiritual energy without getting blown away or inflated. So we can see *why* the purification process has to be deep and real.

And then finally, out of all of this, appears another vital residue. 'Out of the womb of his mother and sister, Isis or mercury,' it is said, 'appears the red king'[4] – a warm, alive residue of earth, signifying rebirth and a new quality of manhood.

And Sol and Luna? What happens to them here? In the beginning, they and their vision are dead. Then the rain comes, falling over their tomb. Slowly there is an awakening, a healing and a softening which the rain brings – one morning, perhaps, as they wake up in bed together. The day stretches in front of them and there is work to do. But a change has taken place: they are not the same people they were, even if outwardly they appear so. Something else is possible now that could not have happened before. And this is *their* work of whitening. For a time their sexual activity is suspended. It is heart-work they have to do now, as the pelican suggests – it is the heart they have to open, or return to. This is going to take time.

In all of this, Luna is important, with her resources of softening, communicating, listening and, above all, feeling, In this, she connects to the *soror mystica* and beyond her, to Lady Alchymia herself. For Sol, the process is a dissolving, for Luna a purifying as a result of the expression of her qualities as a woman.

We can see this again in terms of sulphur and quicksilver. In the beginning, in the *nigredo*, he resists her and they fight. Now he dissolves in her and her element, so his heart – or anger – dissolves in her coolness. But it is more than this. If we can understand sulphur as representing a level of masculine, abstract or conceptual understanding, then it has to 'dissolve' before it can become something that is really alive – something with soul and feeling. So the sun is eclipsed by the moon, if you like.

Solutio is also pictured as women washing sheets – humbling, grounded work that we might rather not do. It strips us of our defences. And it takes a lot of water.

And the water and the fire, as they alternate, change each other's quality. The water becomes more fiery and the fire more watery. We can understand this emotionally and in terms of feeling. More of an actual blending takes place.

When Sol and Luna meet again in closeness, they are changed – and here they are sometimes pictured as birds as well, holding one another, linked as if in a circle, as 'two in one'. Alchemically, they meet at full moon – and again the *Rosarium* is quite specific:

> Cast the female upon the male, and the male shall ascend the female.[5]

So as they make love now, she is on top of him as he lies under her, and of the two birds, *she* is the one who is winged. And then from them emerges a third bird, either a swan or a dove. With the swan, we have royal whiteness; with the dove, we have spirit and soul, lust and grace, in a synthesis that is sacred. Again, this is Mercurius.

As the *Rosarium* states it, emphatically:

> *Thus you have the true Mercurius extracted from the two bodies mentioned above, well-washed and digested. And I swear by God that no other Mercurius exists in the universal way than the one just declared, on which depends the whole philosophy. Who speaks otherwise, speaks false.*[6]

So Sol and Luna are reborn, more tender now and much more vulnerable. Why? Because they know the fire and they know that what holds them together is something beyond them which only openness of heart can penetrate.

And this reveals the real point of the *solutio*, which is that this work on the soul moves inward into what we can't see but can only feel. Here, in this cleansing, we have the potential to regain, as Burckhardt puts it, 'the original purity and receptivity of the soul'. So now the soul is free, *it is alive in our bodies*, and soul and spirit can meet ...

Here is an exercise so you can explore *solutio* for yourself.

You may want to do this exercise in water.

Sitting or lying comfortably, give yourself a moment to breathe again and come back into yourself.

Take a few minutes to reflect on your relationship to water. How aware are you of it? How often do you use it? Do you like or dislike it? What is the feeling it gives you?

Then, if you haven't done so already, close your eyes and go inside – be in your flask.

Then see if you can visualize the moon. Be aware of how you're seeing it. How does it appear to you? How do you feel towards it?

How does its light affect you and your eyes?

Then see if you can connect to a time in your life when you experienced purity or a specific quality of purification.

Where were you (or are you)? What was happening to you and around you?

How did you feel it in your body?

How did it touch you in your feelings or your heart?

How did you experience it in your mind?

Take each question slowly, so you can feel an inner response in your body, feelings and mind.

Now see if an image emerges. Again, allow what wants to come, however strange of unusual it might seem.

Let it form for a moment, and then reflect on it and what it is trying to show you or say to you. Remember you can ask it 'What are you trying to show me or say to me?'

Come back when you're ready and make a drawing of your image along with any notes you can record.

You might like to compare this experience to your previous one in *nigredo*. What are the differences? What are the connections? Try placing your two drawings side by side. How do they look together?

Review your Lesser Work so far. What has it been like in the flask? How in touch have you been with it? And what does your flask need from you now? See if you can take a moment to close your eyes and ask it.

Again, let's look at some of the implications of what is going on here. The *solutio* is really a challenge to purity and it can bring up all we resist in relationship to that. It points deep into our fluid nature – as 60 per cent water, we are, after all, in no way as solid or unchangeable as we seem. At the simplest level, we can experience it every time it rains and changes the day (into 'a soft day', as they say in Ireland). Roger Evans, co-founder of the London Institute of Psychosynthesis, told us during a Summer School gathering about how he'd once been walking in the rain and suddenly decided to take his shirt off, reversing his habitual response, and how freeing that had been. That would be embracing *solutio*.

Solutio also brings us to feeling in a particular way and the experience can be like being stripped naked. As James Hillman puts it in his 'Alchemical Solutions', relating water and tears to salt:

> Felt experience *takes on a radically altered meaning in the light of alchemical salt. We may imagine our deep hurts not merely as wounds to be healed but as salt mines from which we gain a precious essence and without which the soul cannot live.*[7]

That last phrase is telling. It is an encouragement to us to take our feelings seriously as well as personally – rather than as sudden awkward showers that are as quickly covered up with a semblance of sunshine. That would be avoiding *solutio* which actually – like all the stages here – has a will and an agenda of its own.

This agenda is to soften us and bring us in touch with the feminine. This can be a particular challenge to men who fear losing what they imagine to be their strength. But it doesn't mean being limp or flaccid, though we may need to experience that for a time. It means having the courage to be receptive, because this quality lies at the essence of relationship. If I can't feel and allow what is around me, how can I relate to you or expect you to relate to me?

In a very real sense we are going into the unknown here – going out to sea – and the experience can be like swooning or fainting, losing our usual grip on things, feeling in a strange sense of suspension, like snow falling. Watery images – baptism, womb water, seminal fluid, fountain, bath, lake, pool – all come in.[8] We are on a night sea journey somewhere between two places, neither of which we can see. And if we are asleep, we are dreaming – and dreams are particularly relevant here in the realm of Neptune, who rules the unconscious source of dreaming.

Solutio is purification, but again, it is not an easy process. We experience it first through pain and tears, grief that may have been bottled up for years. It is likely to take us into the hurt places that need recognition and healing – even into actual heartbreak, as that may be the only way our hearts can really open.

In every crisis there is an opportunity, however, and as the heat begins to increase, we can see this as an opportunity for expansion: to work, for instance, actively with our depression rather than being a passive victim to it, as *nigredo* often demands. In *solutio* we can start to do something about it (like going to see a good therapist) and then a leavening can take place. We can start to understand where we are and why heartbreak perhaps had to be the case.

We can often fall in love in *solutio* (or equally, out of it) but there can be a difficulty in knowing what is real and what is a dream, something wished for that is either not exactly mutual or not, as yet, real. We haven't actually embodied it yet or made a commitment to it. At the same time, as Marie-Louise von Franz adds on a note of consolation:

> There is no 'should' about it. I think a real spiritual experience
> – I don't know exactly what you have in mind when you say
> that – does become manifest. Mythos means communication.
> If you are overwhelmed by a spiritual experience it itself wants
> you to communicate it, i.e. manifest it; that is the meaning of
> the word mythos. There is no religious experience where there
> is not the need to tell of it; that is natural, but one need not
> add the word 'should'. If it is true, it will become real, its nat-
> ural flow will be into reality.[9]

And that, like love, takes time. Gold takes time and we are not yet in sight of it. Yet, 'as the matter turns white', as the fire increases, we move into more refined areas of feeling and awareness. We are looking at purification within sexuality too – purification of lust into a more tender *love-making*. Purification also leads towards seeing people everywhere no longer just as objects, but as souls walking on a street. You can see the difference immediately – and you can be aware of what it is in you that can see and feel it.

In a higher sense still, as we approach an understanding of the white stone, we find a concentration on and an awareness of our own process – rather than projecting it all onto another person. A woman on one of my workshops,[10] who had done the exercise in this chapter, spoke of it giving her 'candour, emptiness and purity of intent', while another had an extraordinary image of a white bird 'revelling in the movement of air', as she put it. And, as another woman wrote subsequently, in coming in to her true feminine being (which has resulted in her using her full name, Catherine, rather than Katie):

I felt serene, and expanded – as though I filled my skin again and might even burst right out of it. So there was a splendid tension to balance the serenity.

And, as a man in that group also added, 'Love will perceive as never I could.'

This brings us to the white stone itself as a touchstone inside us, transforming the love of power into the *power to love*. So we come to a new appreciation of love, as distinct from manipulation and coercion, a more spiritual love and quality of loving that is 100 per cent more feeling and alive. We start to see that regardless of any other particular individual, we are here to love and to learn to love.

So through the purification of water and fire, we have a White Queen, and a Red King, whose 'fiery calcined earth' is the residue. We have a new kind of man and a new kind of woman – and we have the grounds for something real.

As you review your experience of *solutio*, I want to suggest you ask yourself 'How pure are my intentions?', 'How honest am I allowing myself to be?', 'How much in touch am I with my feelings?' and 'What does love mean to me?' This is the alchemy here. You might want to meditate on that, as well as sharing it with another brother or sister on the path. And if you go out walking now, see if you can find yourself a white stone ...

Collectively, evidence for *solutio* may initially seem less obvious in a world blackened by newsprint, but it is here among all of us who in our different ways hear the call to purify. It is in the feeling we are prepared to put into life – where we see that we can all live a feeling life, whether as artists or architects, doctors or mini-cab drivers.

In the feeling life, inner and outer are one – the 'above' and the 'below' touch. Things no longer just happen *out there* – they happen *in here* as well. We can see this dedication among those of us who are called to a religious life and we can see it more broadly among all of us who recognize that we are leading spiritual lives in which love is the key. This is vastly increasing, as it needs to in every sense – it is becoming more and more a part of our everyday lives as a way of communing with ourselves and each other outside of churches and other official structures. 'My church is my heart,' as I was once moved to say, 'and its roof is the open and unending sky.'

Solutio extends to the body too, in terms of our recognition of the importance of health and cleansing, where what we choose to eat and *not* eat becomes relevant. We can recognize 'solution' here medicinally as well, whether in the form of flower remedies, Chinese herbs or, more graphically, in enema treatment, cleaning the shit out of our guts.

Purification is needed on every level: not just in our thoughts, our feelings and our bodies, but throughout our polluted environment and world. We can see this literally with water we can't even drink – as well as in dead rivers lakes and seas that Greenpeace boats are battling over in their green martyrdom. We can see it in chemical dumping and feel it in the debased language that we speak. We can hear it in the cacophony of noise we generate that drowns out the sound of wind and birdsong, and stops us feeling or thinking anything clearly at all.

Solutio has its shadow side, too, and that is in spiritual inflation (or *superbia*,[11] as the Greeks called it), being too good or too special for this world. *Solutio* can also be linked to narcotic substances, being narcissistic and getting stuck in fantasy or chemical unreality. Here what we tend to see is the water without the fire, the latter part of this stage that not only leads us towards clarity – like a crystal growing suspended in liquid – but also back *out* towards a reality that is still very much earthly. We can see the difference here between what Robert Bly criticizes as the 'soft man',[12] and the Red King. They are not the same at all.

The thing to guard against in *solutio* is staying in the womb for too long. If we do, the water tends to turn bitter. We must actually be reborn, after all. *We must come out of death into Love.*

Albedo Aubade
heart-fire
illumines
eyes meeting
the moon
with a moon
that mirrors
heaven
with heaven

so moon-beams
may ignite
the sun

& huntress
dart flame
from each hair
of his mane

till we learn
from the luminous
ocean we bathe in
the first
distillation
of love

GLENN STORHAUG

THE GREATER WORK

COAGULATIO

The two natures change one another reciprocally, the body 'incorporating' the spirit, and the spirit transmuting the body into a coloured and white spirit ... This is the dissolution of the body, and the fixation of the Spirit, both processes constituting one and the same work.

ARTEPHIUS

This mixture or union cannot be realized without transformation, which means a sublimation of the body, and its reduction into a spiritual form.

ROSARIUM PHILOSOPHORUM

Altogether, sulphur is one of the innumerable synonyms for the prima materia *in its dual aspects, i.e. as both the initial material and the end-product.*

C. G. JUNG

The body has to be spiritualized and the spirit must be incarnated, both things must take place.

MARIE LOUISE VON FRANZ

To desire and to see through desire – this is the courage that the heart requires.

JAMES HILLMAN, THOUGHT OF THE HEART

COAGULATIO

A BMW stripped of paint – khaki under the setting sun,
The slats of sand-coloured road racing forward downhill...

When shall we rise? Oh when shall we rise?

With *coagulatio*, we cross the threshold into the Greater Work – the embodiment of spirit that *nigredo* and *solutio* have prepared in every way. After *solutio* we can't go further 'up': we can't stay 'raised above': we have to come down. Spirit in matter and matter in spirit – matter *becoming* spirit. That is the work now. *Coagulatio* is a coming to earth then, as the wheel turns, a new kind of dying, and of all the stages it specifically reveals the alchemical process as a quest for substance, for substantiality.

Coagulatio returns us to earth in a positive sense. Its earth is warm, it is sensuous. It is the new quality of earth of John's statement in the Book of Revelation:

And I saw a New Heaven and a New Earth.

It is very different from the bitter earth of *nigredo*. Where *nigredo* is sometimes described as a 'cracking of old earth',[1] here we are cracking new earth – we are breaking new ground.

Returning to our key phrase *solve et coagula*, this is the *coagula*, meaning 'to coagulate', 'to congeal', 'to thicken', as well as 'to ground' and 'to enliven'.

As Alexander Sethon and Michael Sendivogius also said in relationship to this:

> *If there were no animal sulphur in man, the mercury of his blood could not be congealed into flesh and bones; and if plants contained no vegetable sulphur, their mercury or water (sap) would not be congealed into leaves and flowers.*[2]

This also suggests another important distinction, which is between transmutation and transformation. We tend to think of transformation alone, as a kind of guaranteed promise of change, without recognizing that for change to be real, it also has to be *physical* – it has to be in the body and at a subtle level of energy. That is transmutation and it comes before transformation itself can take place. Otherwise we may experience release or relief, but not a permanent change.

So *coagulatio* brings us to the body – to matter – to the earth that is all around us, green-gold in the sunlight.

It brings us out of the night, out of dreaming into daylight and awakening.

Its essence is *yellowing*, which is why it is also known as *citrinitas*, from which we derive the word 'citrine', with its connotations of citrus fruit – the fresh yellow of a lemon or the glowing globe of an orange. Its taste is strong, tart, sudden – and full of energy. The yellowing is *creative* energy too, vibrant and alive like the day, and it is in this stage that the masculine principle re-emerges.

After the stripping-away of *solutio*, and the baring of soul there is in it, what we have here is a reclothing in earth that has parallels with the Egyptian rites of Osiris, where the initiate is reclothed as he emerges from the darkness. *Coagulatio* takes place under the sign of Venus and then of Mars, where Venus represents a quality of earth as well as love, as embodied woman, and Mars, with his sword, stands for the redness of fire and strength. Venus and Mars are archetypal feminine and masculine energies here, as they are astrologically. And they have to do with the balance of masculine and feminine in all of us, and the dynamic between them.

Venus and Mars are Luna and Sol at a higher or more expanded level; and what we can see here immediately in terms of the sequence is that Mars follows Venus, as Sol follows Luna.

So we come specifically to the character of Sol. For sulphur is the agent of coagulation. If *solutio* brings us to an awareness of the feminine, the *anima*, then *coagulatio* is a meditation on the masculine. As the *Turba* puts it, suggestively:

> *At the beginning woman is on top of man, and at the end man is on top of woman.*[2]

Here, Sol is raw, only just reborn; he is still impure, and yet he is vital in what he needs to be now and become as the agent of a refined fire and strength. What Luna was, Sol now has to be – and in and through himself as well. But first he has to pass through Venus. He has to go through the element of earth.

Coagulatio is both the first stage of the Greater Work and a preparation for the end or realization of the *whole* Work, which is why we need to explore it thoroughly. Some alchemists, as I've mentioned, actually missed it out, going – as they saw it – straight from the white to the *rubedo* red, raising the temperature to maximum heat. I don't believe it can be missed out, although such impatience is understandable. It would be leaving out a quality of earth, and earthing, that is vital to the Stone and to what the *rubedo* can be for us.

There are a number of phases within the overall stage of *coagulatio* – the first four taking place under Venus and the second four under Mars, after which Sol and Luna reunite again. They are:

separatio

fermentatio
illuminatio
nutrimentum

fixatio
multiplicatio
revificatio

sublimatio

and we will come to each of them in turn.

Images of *coagulatio* include the sower, or alchemist-or-sower, scattering what he has gained in *solutio* onto the 'foliate earth' in the form of fermenting gold. 'Foliate' here means 'leaf-covered'; suggestive of autumn or the red time of year. It is an image of letting go. Then we have the snake, the *serpens mercurialis* who is Mercurius again in another of his animal guises, twisting round, encircling and piercing the lunar egg of *solutio* in the flask, cleaving it till it cracks and re-forms as the sun. We have bird images of ascent that include the swan, giving way to the eagle who can fly

nearer the sun and, coming down, we have piercing solar rays of naked ultraviolet sunlight, sometimes shown as birds with little bows and arrows. These solar rays are rays of the Spirit infusing the body. We can experience them simply by sunbathing, feeling the prickle of heat on our skin. We have the rainbow connecting Heaven and Earth that this stage is the bridge to; we have dawn and sunrise – all images of solar return. We have the pelican (as in *solutio*), suggesting the ongoing work of feeling, experiencing feeling *in the body* now. And over and beyond all this, we have the New Earth itself, emerging like a continent from the waters of *solutio*, at first like islands in a stream, then becoming a land mass ... earth washed by water returning to light.

Coming back to Sol and Luna, another turn of events takes place. It begins with a descent. He softens inside her, and she withdraws her legs. He lies there, perhaps face down, with his head on her belly or to one side in the after-silence, and he begins to fall, to sink down. It is a moment of unexpected exhaustion beyond elation.

He doesn't say anything. She lies back. As the *Rosarium* has it:

> Here Sol is buried and overflowed
> With Mercurius philosophorum.[4]

He is sinking, he is sinking to earth, as the snake slides into the flask. Above the couple, their androgynous form begins to separate into its two halves and as Sol sinks, Luna rises. She goes north while he stays, perhaps far away. She is out of reach, not contactable by phone. They both are.

This is *separatio* and it is the first movement that takes place. It is one of differentiation, because it is about Sol and Luna individually as man and woman, and so while the focus of this stage is on Sol, it is Luna's work as well. But they have to do it separately. *Consciously or not, she knows this – and she needs him to know it. Because it is through this that she begins to call on his power as a man.*

fermentatio

This post-coital phase, where mercury and sulphur are separated, initiates *fermentatio* (literally, 'fermentation') where we come on to the stone itself. As the snake begins to coil and twist, tightening its hold on the shell inside the flask, there is an experience of constriction as well as sinking, of being surrounded and bound, hedged about on all sides. In this *solve* part of the *coagula*, the white lunar stone begins to dissolve as it is joined to its ferment which is gold. This ferment is the yellowing, and it is through this – 'little by little' as it is said – that the coagulation in all its stages takes place. So the stone's ferment yellows the whiteness – and through this the silver that the whiteness represents begins to become gold.

This is the first action of sulphur: corrosive, dissolving and coming to matter. It clarifies the essential male energy seen as semen which the illustration below names in the centre of its triangle.

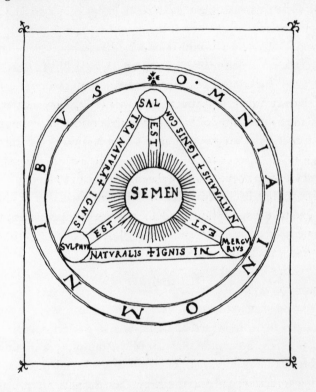

And as Senior comments in the *Rosarium*:

> *This is the preparation which they call the change and the division and this on account of its change in the preparation, from stage to stage, from infirmity to power, from the gross to the fine and subtle. In such a manner the semen alone converts itself under the influence of the matrix of the natural preparation, from thing to thing, until from this is formed the perfect man from that which was his root and beginning.*[5]

This gives us a clue to the real progress of Sol through *coagulatio* as a working through the masculine and it helps us to understand what this descent is about. This dying here is to create a richer fertility. The analogy of the grain of wheat falling to earth in John 12:23–4 is a useful one. As he says, 'but if it dies, it bringeth forth much fruit.' We can understand this in ourselves in terms of our contact with the ground. It is through our earthiness that we are fertile – that is why we need to enter into it.

So, for a man, this is an acquaintance with his semen: his own power, his own perception, his own real way of discerning things.

And for the masculine in a woman, too, it can be seen in terms of her own fertile clarity, in terms of her own will, her ability to focus, to take responsibility and direct herself, remembering that we are under the sign of Venus here.

illuminatio

The second stage, known as *illuminatio* ('illumination') brings a green-gold light, in which the gold is said to first appear. And again we have a paradox. Sol is still in the process of sinking (sometimes he is pictured going into a well) and the snake is starting to actually pierce the shell. Yet there is illumination, light. What does this mean? Johannes Fabricius puts it beautifully when he describes how the alchemist feels at this point:

> The alchemist's voluntary sacrifice in the citrinitas of the riches he has gained in the albedo reflects the inexorable process of alchemical transformation compelling the adept to ever new adjustments, unexplored procedures, unknown attitudes.[6]

There is a real sense in which we are in the unknown here, in the sense of it being the reverse of our expectation. *Illuminatio* is pictured in terms of piercing – the solar rays, the arrows – and of purgation in which 'the moist earthly body yields to the dry'. The 'dry' here is the sun and Heaven (or the 'above'), while the moist and earthly is the body (the 'below') and this is taking place while the stone is increasingly being yellowed.

This piercing is an awakening of Sol to himself – an awakening of consciousness in which he begins to become his own light. Sometimes Luna is shown pointing the bow *at* him and this gives us a further clue. The experience of criticism or anything that is sharp forces us back on ourselves. It may be the last thing we want. But in it, and through it, we awaken – and this awakening is the light. So Luna, wherever she is, may be awakening Sol to himself too – and as a result of this awakening and its re-orientation, there can be *an ascent in awareness*. So we have the birds: the swan that becomes the eagle reaching up to the source of light, with the sun on his wings and in his eyes. The eagle here is also a symbol of masculine as well as spiritual consciousness, very different from the white swan.

So Sol is waking up – and it's painful. It is slow, too. He may even be a bit out of his depth, caught between reaction and understanding. This slowness is a feature of *coagulatio* as a whole, particularly in these earlier phases. It is a cooler process altogether. As one inscription reads:

When you see the white colour, cool down your work, and you will arrive from the lunar to the solar colour.[7]

And as another one adds:

So great is the medicine, that it will produce gold.[8]

This medicine is the awakening of consciousness that transmutes the body, linking the 'above' and the 'below'.

nutrimentum

This transmutation under Venus brings us to *nutrimentum*, also referred to as *cibatio*, which means 'feeding the new'. This phase is about nourishment and here it is said that 'the red sulphur [Sol] is digested by the silvery moon after its purgation'. Sol has sunk even deeper here and the snake's movements are rupturing the egg in a myriad of tiny fissures. As the *Rosarium* says:

> Here Sol in turned black, becoming with
> Mercurius philosophorum *one heart*.

Sol's blackness is almost *nigredo*-like – and there is a link, but it is different. Here it is more like depression, being brought low, constrained by physical form. But then what takes place is *a feeding* – in the sense of Sol feeding from the feminine, from what Luna has left inside him. What becomes clear is that *nutrimentum* is an awakening of a man to his own feminine, not as *anima* but as nourishment. Deeper than that, what we also have is Sol feeding from the earth herself. He is finding his heart of earth, the feeling that really embodies him by connecting him to matter as something living and warm, warm as the earth soaked with sun, just as all food is grown and filled with sunlight.

So here what we need to do is open our hearts to the earth. And then again we will find Mercurius, who is always the energy of life.

So under Venus, Sol is both grounded and awakened. His heart is opened to himself and his feeling is earthed. He begins to become himself, his 'own man' as we say. This is Luna's gift to him after he has surrendered and dissolved in her. And beyond her, it is the gift of Venus, too, who stands for real as well as loving woman. Sol grows through this, as you can imagine. But it is only half of the story. Under Venus, the sun is said to show as a copper sun.

There is gold, but it is still 'unstable and coarse'.[9] It requires the second half of *coagulatio* that brings us to Mars.

fixatio

Mars signifies the beginning of the solar life where Sol comes into his own, and the balance begins to tilt to the other side.

The balance between masculine and feminine and feminine and masculine in alchemy, is very finely and thoroughly articulated, just as scales you would weigh actual gold in.[10] Sol, or sulphur, without quicksilver, or Luna, creates rigidity and quicksilver without sulphur results in dissipation. Now we are weighing in Sol and his gift to Luna of his true and essential maleness.

The temperature rises in the flask and we come to *fixatio* (literally, 'fixing', 'solidifying').

So we have *coagula*. In this phase mutable silver is said to acquire the constancy of gold or gold-likeness. Constancy is a key word here, when we think of constancy of feeling and of standing our ground – as men, with a certain rock-likeness in the heart. This is the beginning of what alchemists call the solar life – or of *manhood* as we would understand it now.

And it is about womanhood in the sense of a woman finding her masculine or *animus* positively and not externalizing it solely onto an outer man or father figure. So in gender terms, Luna's journey mirrors Sol. It is what she needs to accomplish within herself.

Lunar light becomes solar light and in the flask as the heat rises, the stone begins to redden. This coincides with the evaporation of its watery or moist quality (remembering that 'moist' signifies Earth, and 'dry' Heaven). Within Sol, this is a coming to the centre – to the centre of himself and what he can give, literally by standing in his own fire.

As the *Aurea catena* states it:

> The nearer a subject is to the centre, the more strongly it is
> fixed, if only it is not hindered by the copious and continually
> rising moisture.[11]

The sense here is of needing to go on: to not be held back by dwelling in a negative way on feelings or pain.

And then, like a lightning flash, as the snake coils, twisting with its tail in its mouth, the contents of the flask catch fire – and in the blaze we have the strength of the rising sun, rising Sol, rising power.

The above touches the below and the below answers to the above.

Soul and spirit are beginning to come together.

multiplicatio

This answering is greeted by rain from Heaven – and this is the image of *multiplicatio* (literally, 'multiplying'). This stage signifies expansion – an expansion of potency like the rising sun's rays – and abundance or plenty. William Blake's naked man with his hands spread open in 'Glad Day' is a good image of *multiplicatio*. There is something unashamed about it. It is entirely and disarmingly natural. It is what a glad man greets the rain with.

In the flask, the sulphur is said to be no longer fermenting in the stone, but fixing it by 'multiplying in its earth', so that here – with energy from the rain, or the above (i.e., spirit) – sulphur expands as the stone is transmuted ... and the snake's movements finally restore the egg to a golden globe.

Light fills the flask, between the above and the below which is the heart: the sun as the strength of the heart.

revificatio

Now the snake dies, having done its work, and is revealed as Sol's own sexuality, in its impure form of compulsion, 'having to'. This is the *revificatio* ('resurrection') phase. What rises through this is not his penis, but his spiritual strength *where his sexuality becomes the whole of his body*. So we have containment, as men, and an aliveness that comes right through us. We have light.

And as women? We have a fire that we can contain that comes from solar strength. This is a woman's independence, emotionally and sexually, that can be more naturally her own here.

It is at this point that the body is 'completely penetrated by the incombustible sulphur'[12] which corresponds to a terrific inner strengthening, not only of the body as we know it, but the body seen as a vessel, just as the flask is. The spirit can even seem to be submerged in the body and this has been referred to (again by Burckhardt) as 'the outermost coagulation' that comes right at the end of Mars.

We may still experience ourselves as being alone here, but it is at this point that Luna comes closer, as if magnetized by an invisible force. That magnetism is Sol and what he has achieved in himself – and she, being a woman, senses it without the need for speech. She senses it in what he is. And it touches her.

So we can see, through all of this, that Luna goes through Mars as Sol has Venus. We can read everything we have read for Sol for Luna as well, in her own light as a woman, and in what takes place in the flask with the stone. That is their *coagulatio* independently, just as we can see it being ours as men or women.

And now, the stone is said to be 'fluent': articulate, coagulate, coming without difficulty.

sublimatio

And when Sol and Luna come back together? They are no longer alone. They bring the above and the below that is Heaven and Earth with them, as individual as they are in themselves now. They meet in blood – they are often pictured in a bath of blood – so they are meeting in the reality of feeling and body that signifies the final phase of reddening here as a shared thing. Their meeting reveals what all their work has been for: to enable a *greater* thing to come between them, to witness, guide and nourish them. They are both enriched by their separation and here – in *perfectio* as it is called – they are pictured together, standing individually on earth under the sun and the stars, connected in their bodies to soul and to the instinctual, with spirit reaching above them, between them, just as Heaven and Earth connect in reality. And above them, in the solar centre, appears the sign of Mercurius in an upward-pointing triangle that is the 'third point' or apex between them:

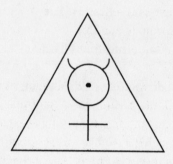

So as they make love now, the upward and downward-pointing triangles of the Seal of Solomon (*see p.8*) begin to merge like a star, a star that has no name and while they may be Sol and Luna, they could by yin and yang as well, beyond themselves, as they return to the centre and the third body that is theirs – but not *just* theirs, like a precious possession; it is something larger that they share in now that is grace-given. As another verse inscription reads:

> The things that are in the realms above
> Are also in the realms beneath.
> What Heaven shows is often found on earth.
> Fire and flowing water are contraries,
> Happy thou if thou canst unite them.[13]

This is the *sublimatio* ('sublimation'): it is a love-making of heightened sensitivity that is closer to Tantra, in which the lovers' awareness spreads inwardly to Heaven and outwardly to Earth. They are open-eyed, clear-eyed, unillusioned, free, as capable of being alone as together.

So they are renewed as Red King and White Queen at the threshold of a further, final step. As Pearl S. Buck adds, significantly:

It is not the same love that one feels in youth or the same love that one may feel in middle age, but it's a very special rewarding love, the love that gives and asks for nothing, and whatever comes back is pure gold.[14]

So in *coagulatio* there is a movement through the *solve* and *coagula* of descent, of sinking down, and then of rising, of reconnection and return. It is circular in this sense – as the snake is, swallowing its own tail – as well as being a particular evolution in the process we are in *as* a whole. It prepares us for the embodiment of spirit. Before this spirit has to come *right into the body*, or 'right down through' as some psychics say.[15] So it is a strengthening of the vessel to take the new wine – or the fullness of spirit – that would otherwise shatter us. Finally, and simply, it is incarnation – it is really being *in* a body – which is why of all the four main stages of the Work it is the longest. And the point of it? It is to reclaim the original purpose of the body and to understand why – with the best will in the world – we are human here and we don't yet have wings.

Now here is another exercise so you can explore this stage for yourself – with or without your partner, lover of friend.

You may want to do this exercise sitting outside. If not, then I'd suggest you take a walk afterwards so you can feel your feet on the ground and absorb the energy of the earth through them.

Take a moment to sit and connect to your breathing.

Then close your eyes. Really connect to your body as you do. Be in it and be aware of how it is feeling.

Then take a minute to imagine light in and around the crown of your head, coming from the sun. Be aware of the quality of the light – and of the sun if you are sitting in it.

Then begin to bring the light down, slowly, feeling what happens as it comes into your body, down your throat, across the tops of your shoulders, into your chest area, down your arms ... into your belly ... to the ends of your fingers, into your thighs ... through your kneecaps, down your calves into your ankles and feet, and into the ground.

Feel it infusing you in every cell and be aware of any resistance(s) you meet.

Then bring your attention to your genital area. How connected do you feel to it? What is the energy there?

Then bring your awareness up towards your heart. Pause again there. How is your heart feeling? What connection do you feel between it and your sexuality? Can you see one?

Then move back up to your head.

Just see if this experience of the light, or of your heart and sexuality reminds you of anything in your life – an event or a phase. What comes to mind? What does it feel like?

See if an image for the experience comes forward. Can you see what area of your body it is pointing to? Be specific here.

You can ask it to indicate an area for you that may need healing.

Then reflect for a moment or two on what that might be saying to you about your relationship to your body: what it is and what it could be.

Come back when you're ready and make notes as fully as you can. (You can of course draw if it is useful too.)

And then, walk at whatever pace you feel inside yourself. Feel your body, its rhythm and movement, its breath and its needs, wherever you are.

How are you seeing the earth now?

How are you feeling it and sensing it?

Is there any particular connection you want to make to it? And can you?

As you review your experience of *coagulatio*, see if you can evaluate what your relationship to matter has been. How in touch with it are you? How balanced is your relationship to it in terms of your inner and spiritual life? And how sensual, rather than sexual, do you allow yourself to be? See what images or memories come to mind along the green-gold (and red-gold) thread of your days, and see how they relate to your experience of being in physical form.

In addition, you may like to circle back and look at your experience of each of the phases within this overall stage. This would be a valuable exercise in itself. Give yourself some reflective time with each of them, check what your feeling is with them, how you see them in yourself, *and where they bring you to in your body* in terms of where you need to coagulate further. This would deepen your awareness of this stage as a whole.

The essence of *coagulatio* is all about 'earthing' – grounding, embodying, incarnating – and this is why it follows *solutio*. It is a gateway to the outside world that we are a part of every time we start our cars or lift a forkful of food to our mouths. So it opens us out – out to the haulage of articulated lorries, the yellow helmets of motorway or bypass construction workers, and the yellow of JCBs shovelling newly broken earth. Matter.

But not matter alone. Spirit is there as well and *matter revealed as spirit*.

Marie Louise von Franz clarifies *coagulatio* in conversation, in one of her lectures, drawing out its implications for all of us. She asks one of her audience members:

How would you look at that? The body, the material thing, becomes spiritualized and the spirit in turn becomes concrete. What would that mean in practice?
 The end of the split between body and spirit.
 Yes, but what does that look like?

It would be a totally different attitude towards the body.
In what way?
It would be putting the analytical or spiritual experience
into actual life.

Yes, that would be solidifying the spirit. If you apply a psy-
chological realization, then you incarnate what was spiritual.
If you recognize something as right and put it into action then
it becomes real. Now what would the other part involve?

An attitude of consciousness which retires in part from
spontaneous experience, while looking at it symbolically – a
kind of spiritualization of experience.[16]

That last phrase is significant. It suggests that in reality we can
only see matter with the eyes of spirit if we are to see what earth
and earthly experience really are. This reverses our reductive
habit of seeing things separately so that we never actually *feel*
them; and it calls for the end of the dualism that has made such
a mockery of our potential and creative lives.

So in *coagulatio*, we come down. We have to come down from
our pride so that this connection can be achieved and the split
can be healed. Interestingly it is what Sol – or the masculine –
specifically has to go through.

Coagulatio is a coming down into form, too, just as an idea has
to be put into practice or an image made visible through artistic
expression. Coagulating is a vital part of any artist's journey, in
learning the craft. Seamus Heaney puts it well in his finely con-
centrated poem 'The Earth House', that is moulded or cast in the
shape of what it is describing:

> *I was four but I turned four hundred maybe*
> *Encountering the ancient dampish feel*
> *Of a clay floor. Maybe four thousand even.*
>
> *Anyhow, there it was. Milk poured for cats*
> *In a rank puddle-place, splash-darkened mould*
> *Around the terra cotta water-crock.*

Ground of being. Body's deep obedience
To all its shifting tenses. A half-door
Opening directly into starlight.

Out of that earth house I inherited
A stack of singular, cold memory-weights
To load me, hand and foot, in the scale of things.[17]

And as we come down, we find that objects have a silent feeling life of their own. This is one of the qualities of the coagulate stone – this recognition, this contact. Or, as poet Paul Matthews adds in one of his directives for creative writing in poetic form: 'Start anywhere./Start with a blue chair'. It's useful advice: starting immediately from whatever is around you.[18]

Coagulatio is a reclothing, as we've said, and in it there is a re-connecting to ego after the stripping of *solutio*, but in a positive sense now that relates to expression and the use of the will – to actively being who we are and what we are becoming. In the Venus phase, particularly in *nutrimentum*, it also brings us to a reclaiming of our instinctual being and through that to a recognition of the energy we need in order to heal and be well. This remarkable dream, given to me by Lucy Lidell, herself a well known writer and healer, illustrates this memorably:

I am sitting beside a lake. I press one of my breasts and find there is milk there. I try the other one and milk flows out of that breast too. I am amazed. And then, reaching down, I discover I have a magnificent penis, fully 8 or 9 inches long. I think, 'I must be pregnant.' A nurse says that it won't go to term, however, as my pulse rate is too fast or unusual in some way.

This was one of the most profoundly physical dreams I've ever had – I can still remember the sensation of extraordinary pleasure...

At the time of the dream, she knew far less about our subject than she realized; afterwards she commented on her sense of completeness and continuing wonder: 'It's as if I've got everything I need here.'

This also brings us to an awareness of gender and the balance of masculine and feminine within ourselves. It also has to do with *finding the other in ourselves* in terms of our own completeness as individuals. This is coagulate work. As another woman, whom I have already quoted, more recently confided in a letter:

> *I have been so focused on the feminine, the womanly, and yes even the 'queenly' quality of Catherine, I hadn't given any thought to her masculinity. I wasn't ready then to relate to that aspect of her. But I feel it now, as the part of me who stands up very straight, looks the world in the eye and faces it head on; with a new self-assuredness.*

This is Luna, with her red lion, and deservedly. Meanwhile another man, in one of my groups, spoke simply of having to walk down a muddy path alone to find his healing.

In all of this we can see a change in relationship as Luna and Sol do their work, a change that involves differentiation. They both draw back so as to make the circles of who they both are more complete. For many of us, this is contemporary, this 'desert journey' where a couple are brought to face their differences in character and needs. The challenge it creates is one of both discrimination and honesty. The space between is for individual realization. As Thomas Moore remarks in *Care of the Soul*:

> *As we become transparent, revealed for exactly who we are and not who we wish to be, then the mystery of human life as a whole glistens momentarily in a flash of incarnation. Spirituality emanates from the ordinariness of this human life made transparent by lifelong tending to its nature and fate.*[19]

It is no accident, I think, that the reunion of Sol and Luna is said to take place in Aquarius, which symbolizes everything that is new and can be newly conceived. And, as Moore adds, invitingly:

> *The ultimate marriage of spirit and soul,* animus *and* anima, *is the wedding of heaven and earth, our highest ideals and ambitions united with our lowliest symptoms and complaints.*[20]

Coagulatio takes us deeper, too, into the realm of commitment – to ourselves – and even sacrifice that acknowledging our limitations is also related to. It deepens the ground and our awareness of the ground we are standing on as ourselves – with all that means in choosing to be ourselves. There is destiny and there is choice, and the relationship between them is a paradox and a mystery – but at moments in our lives, choice, and the need to choose, become clear as an imperative we can experience as spirit, or coming from spirit. And of course, in every choice between things, a loss is involved. This is closer that infusion of spiritual energy we see from *fixatio* onwards in the reddening. Another woman, on doing a visualization connected to this stage, found herself 'shaping herself' and her image was of an altar that became an anvil, as she said, 'for the spirit to descend on as fire'. Her subsequent life experience proved the truth of this in every way in terms of the strength she has needed to remain true to herself and her calling, both in her art and in her primary relationship.

And, as Lionel Snell, magician and writer, says of his discovery here that links us both back and forward in the process:

> *My own experience of this stage was of a dream of scraping tawdry paint away and discovering a beautiful diamond and feeling great peace and power. My* nigredo *has generated a sense of total emptiness and I had yearned for something to fill that vacuum. Instead this dream transmuted emptiness into flawlessness: a colourless gem that was all colour, the clarity which was most sought after. In my emptiness I had uncovered the hardest and most enduring substance on earth.* [21]

Or we can think, enormously and simply (and at every Easter) of Christ on the cross with his heart open, human and suffering and timeless in his gesture of redemption.

Coagulatio also brings us to our values too. What do we value? We are each invited to ask the Grail question: 'Whom does it serve?' Here the ego is in service of the Self, both in ourselves (in terms of who we truly are) and for the world. Alchemists have a saying that is as rich now as it was when it was first coined: 'Deal in the market place, but always with true gold'.[22] That can apply to all of us, whatever we are doing, or are about to do, in the world.

But *coagulatio* has a suffering all of its own, too, and as the longest stage in the process it is also the longest journey – it is where most of us live most of the time in our adult lives. And at mid-life particularly, we can get tired, tired of it. As Jung said, 'Individuation doesn't make you any younger.' But it can be worse than that. There can be the feeling that it is all *too* long – and where, after all this, have I actually got to? What have I achieved? Here we find the temptation to give up, to roll over and sleep, that coincides with a feeling of being submerged in the body. There may be a recognition of betrayal, too, which can be painful and which needs a lot of support: 'I know what I'm supposed to do – and I haven't been doing it.' This is a particular kind of darkness before the dawn.

Another kind of suffering, of course, is illness, so common to our experience now. This brings us into the body in a forceful way – a way we can't easily escape. Illness holds the shadow side of life that many of us don't want to look at: it holds the soul in a world that is brutally out of touch with it. Yet it also holds the potential for regeneration – into what we *are* rather than what we are *not*, or are no longer. Like death, it is a reaper, as our previous way of being and our identification with that is taken from under our feet.

As Kat Duff puts it in *The Alchemy of Illness*, following her protracted experience of CFIDS (an illness like ME):

Now that I am – hopefully – through the worst of it, I feel very lucky and eternally grateful for the hands that helped me through those straits to reclaim some lost parts of myself. I cannot forget that those places and my capacity to choose them exist within me, nor can I forget what I have learned about my own fragility and that of the world, so the prayers continue. At the same time, I feel more solid, as though finally standing on both my feet for the first time in my life, as if the pale outline of myself had at last been filled in with color. This combination of fragility and strength is just one of the many curious contradictions that come true in the midst of illness. As the alchemists often said, the 'sun and its shadow' complete the work.[23]

'The sun and its shadow' – its shadow is coagulate, it is matter, it is what we can't deny any more than we can deny death if we want to really have the experience, the beauty and the gift of a heart-opened life.

Collectively, we can see coagulation in every aspect of earthly life. It operates in two ways; in an old and a new way, both of which correspond to the transmutation of sulphur and of Sol himself. It is in its most obvious raw form in building, engineering, industry and technical production – we can hear it on a factory floor, hammering in the air and grinding in conveyor belts, clocking in and clocking out. All of this is raw Sol: raw daylight, Apollonian like the sun. And there is transmutation of substances here, whether metallic or pharmaceutical. Mixtures are made, parts put together, advertisements cover hoardings … *coagulatio* is real life – or at least the agreed model of reality we go by.

And of course there is a flaw in all of this, just as there is in Sol himself. The flaw is in his sulphurous rawness and all the limitations that entails. It is not simply a question of materialism (alchemy is material, too): it is a blindness that comes out of seeing matter as just matter, simultaneously negating it by view-ing it as merely two-dimensional and being totally reliant on it.

We can see this blindness as soon as we consider the ecological crisis we are in. For all our apparent earthliness and earthiness, we are not really in touch with the earth at all other than as a Mother to be used and abused. We are out of touch with it be-cause we are out of touch with feeling – inwardly, and so out-wardly as well. We have use, mechanism, practicality – but no real circulation of energy founded on awareness and respect, feel-ing and love.

This blindness is also apparent everywhere from racism to drunken pub brawls and football stadium nightmares. It's earth-ly, alright, and it's hellish.

Alchemists have understood what we have yet to understand: *that you can't truly have Earth unless you have Heaven as well.* And why? Because you have no heart or eyes to see it.

So we are slowly beginning to recognize that our experience here is a School of Earth. A playground, yes, but also a school that requires us to become adult while there is still time. So the question comes: 'What does it really mean to be here?' The answer as quickly follows: '*It means to be present*'. Part of this involves our humility – a capacity to see our real size. In *The Coming of the Cosmic Christ*,[24] radical theologian Matthew Fox reminds us that the root of the word 'humility' is *humus*, meaning 'earth', and entering *into* earth is what we do when we coagulate consciously. *Fermentatio, illuminatio* and *nutrimen-tum* are all extremely rich phases when we see them like this – they are ecological in the deepest sense: 'deep ecology' meaning, as it must mean, what is also *in* us.

Green is the colour here – the colour of Nature and of the heart, too – green leading on to gold. This is what the Green movement is broadly for. Now its aims are increasingly within reach with recycled paper, bottle banks, organic farming and per-maculture, as well as tree planting, impending electrical cars and larger projects designed to heal and rebalance the environment.

Also, many young people today, growing up without either the relative luxury or security of what we once knew, want the earth. Travellers, Donga tribe members, motorway protesters – these are the children of *coagulatio*, modern world pagans wearing the khaki of the natural world with their old trucks and buses, their lovers and their animals, moved on from site to site, rejected by an establishment that is entirely unconscious of what it is denying. The savage legal and media attention they have attracted shows the extent of our lack of understanding of what they represent. They are the vulnerable seeds of a new world – seeds which in more settled and protected form are appearing as communities, like islands in a floating sea of link roads and agribusiness. Like all seeds, some will sprout and flourish and others will die – but the impetus toward community is here and it is not going to leave us. Many of us are feeling a growing restlessness that has to do with dreams of new ways of living. We don't simply want to live in jobs, and we don't want to be slaves to bricks and mortar: we want clear air and space to be, work, breathe and live. This is alongside the sense that we belong together as soul friends.

This is global, too. It is the other side of *nigredo*. It is coming; it is work-in-progress. And there is more here as well, which has to do with what the Earth itself is going through as it becomes a *New* Earth, ascending, as it were, to Heaven (remembering the latter stages of the process here, from *revificatio* onwards). Earth is ascending, not only in importance, but in actuality as we begin to ascend in ourselves, with all the lightening that brings as well as the allowing of space and freedom to one another, with grace as well as humour.

And as we come into feeling, we begin to see that *matter is as we see it* – it is not one thing that is solid and immovable. We know this scientifically, but now we can experience it personally. The whole physical world is permeated with feeling, as the breeze stirs through sunlit beech leaves and the gnats swarm, soft brown ... and it is also suffused with what we *can't* see, or yet see – though some of us perceive it as colour, shape and energy. This 'other country' has been the province of shamans, mystics and psychics. Now at this point in our evolution it is open to all of us if we choose to enter into it and work for it. The gates are open.

As we lighten, as we experience more connection on every level of our being, we become *new-minded*. We become more used to our intuition, with its flashes and promptings, and we become more aware of our own authority and our own sense of being guided. We participate in the adventure that life is and was meant to be.

But most of all we come into love as our most natural state, as the most natural place in the world to be. And as we come into love, we begin to see what being 'in love' can really mean, not just as something romantic and exclusive, but a reality among all of us in all the circles that we are a part of, near and far. 'Love is the work and love is the return', as I once heard it from somewhere other than my physical mind.

As we become ourselves, our lives become a part of that greater life which the greater Work indicates. This is the difference between living in ego and living in the 'I' or Self that I am and we are.

This Self[25] is the threshold that is the love in us and between us. And it is the threshold we cross when we die. It is the same. And if we look at our lives from this place we start to see what we have come here to be, and what entering humanness has always meant and will always mean: giving our essence depth and compassion, and finding and forging the form for the qualities and gifts we have brought with us so we use and fulfil them.

This is 'the work of the sun', in soul and spirit, above and below, in all of us.

And its shadow walks with us every step of the way ...

The Crystallisation Process

The crystallisation process is symbolised by the building of the treasure-house by two poor laborers. They are in rags, but these are clean rags. The rich alchemist who has not gained his riches by alchemy strolls by. What is that celestial perfume? It accompanies the crystallisation and formation of the wonder-working stone. But the tower is empty and as yet unroofed, like a vast chimney. Is this smell a property of the building-stones, white granite from Penryn? His laborers who earn two coins a day each, slowly secure the cap-stone, and the shaft falls dark. The wonderful smell is stronger now. The rich man falls to his knees and appears to be praying, but he is sniffing the planks of the floor, wondering if the smell comes up from the earthen foundations; perhaps some jasmine stealthily growing in a few chinks of sunlight let through into a dark cellar. The laborers are descending their ladder, which they have had to hire for one coin. They are anxious to get it back by sun-down. The rich alchemist gets to his feet and fumbles for their coins. As the money passes he understands that the wonderful smell they have bestowed on his useless treasure-house is the natural sweat of their building it.

PETER REDGROVE

SEVEN

THE GREATER WORK

RUBEDO

For your heavenly father is love.
For your earthly mother is love.
For the son of man is love.
THE ESSENE GOSPEL OF PEACE

This day, this day, this, this,
The Royal Wedding is.
THE CHYMICAL WEDDING OF CHRISTIAN ROSENCREUTZ

But one cannot know the procedure unless it be a gift of God,
or through the instruction of a most experienced Master: and
the source of it all is the Divine Will.
LAURENTIUS VENTURA

Thou wilt never make from others the One that thou seekest,
except there first be made one thing of thyself.
GERARD DORN

The duration of the Work depends on the amount of personal
stuff to be worked through.
PATRICK HARPUR

All energy, used correctly, relates to Love.
BOB MOORE

RUBEDO

Your hair gold like an aureole – your face flushed shining
And a curling autumn leaf drifting down in the wind ...

'Everything comes from the One and returns to the One, by the One, for the One' reads the alchemical axiom that in every sense belongs to this final stage. *Rubedo* brings us to Oneness. It points to completion – completion and release. Unity would be another word for it. Synthesis also.

Rubedo also corresponds to a quantum leap, both in consciousness and realization, because the unitive dimension is not something we can grasp with our usual minds, by definition. We have to go beyond them. We can only begin to see and feel the *rubedo* in a place that this stage itself invites us to, a place where mind and feeling are brought together, fused, fixed forever in a way that is permanent and which relates to what is really real, true and heart-awakened in us. *Rubedo* is simply the embodiment of spirit that we have come all this way for.

Glimpses of the spirit are glimmers of *rubedo*, whether inwardly or outwardly. W. B. Yeats describes a wonderful epiphany in his poem 'Vacillation', in which he is touched in this way, suddenly and unexpectedly in a completely ordinary situation:

My fiftieth year had come and gone,
I sat, a solitary man,
In a crowded London shop,
An open book and an empty cup
On the marble table-top.

While on the shop and street I gazed
My body of a sudden blazed;
And twenty minutes more or less
It seemed, so great my happiness,
That I was blessèd and could bless.[1]

'My body of a sudden blazed': that is a phrase to hold on to here as a recognition, or a wish, or both. We stand on the threshold. It is a little like the feeling you may get walking in through the main door of a cathedral and looking up at the high vaulted chamber of the nave ... and at stone that is not grey now, but red – like a vast cathedral of the heart.

We are in it and it is all around us. And it can be so vast sometimes it can seem out of reach like a vanishing dream.

But we are still in it *because it is inside us too*, just as our hearts are always beating, pumping blood round through all the arteries and veins of our bodies, whether we are aware of it or not. And the secret here is also to *ask* for the spirit in an active moment of prayer or meditation. And perhaps as you stand by the side of a lane looking up at a tall ivy-clad tree, a breeze lifts out of nowhere, rippling in all the leaves for a clear moment like an answer before it fades into calm stillness again, and what it seems to say is 'I am with you.' We are graced, or can be, but we need to ask too – and that is what we tend to forget.

The essence of *rubedo* is the reddening that we have already begun to see in *coagulatio*, the ruby red that its name suggests, a vivid 'sparkling red vermilion' that is also suggestive of living blood. It is the colour of autumn and is a royal colour here too, indicating this stage as the crown of the process in which we come into what it means to *be* royal. The other colour here, which the red is related to, is purple: a colour specifically associated with the Spirit in its highest form, for instance in the robe worn by Jesus, 'King of the Jews', in his interview with Pontius Pilate. So purple – or *iosis*, as it is referred to – is the crown too.

In *rubedo* everything comes together and, in so doing, enters a different dimension. Above and below, Heaven and Earth, meet and marry. There is a sense of suspension here as well as timelessness – just as there is in all those moments when we experience ourselves as being outside time, or when time itself actually slows. This is both an inner and an outer reality – a reality both within and beyond the reality we generally know, where a quality of deep time opens. Time 'then' and time 'now' are suddenly continuous, or co-extensive: distances dissolve as we remember this quality that appears then as the heart-thread, the heart-essence of centuries. It is a dimension where *everything is still alive*, and is available to our expanded sense and minds.

Every level is present here, and because alchemy is about wholeness there is a paradox at the heart of the *rubedo*. There is marriage but there is also death. And the extraordinary is also revealed as the ordinary, that is everywhere if we could only see it.

This seeing, this clarity, corresponds to the sign this stage takes place under: the sun, the radiant sun as gold light and centre where the Spirit is said to be victorious. We have come in from Saturn (in the *nigredo*) finally to the sun.

The sun's symbol of the dot surrounded by a circle – which is also the Egyptian hieroglyph for it – signifies manifestation where the finite or incarnate dot (you or I) is surrounded by the infinite. It is the strongest possible expression of what it means to be centred and, in being so, to be in a position to embody the Spirit, that is infinite. *No* dot, no centre, would mean no manifestation. Equally, no circle would mean no spirit. This symbol also points us vitally towards a *oneness in ourselves*:

That is the sun. Two other planets are associated here. The first is Jupiter (as in *solutio*), signifying expansion or expanded consciousness, and the second is Uranus (discovered in 1781), which signifies inspiration and a sudden leap or change, with its lightning-like bolt of electricity that is both fire and light at the same time. Uranus is innovative, shocking and new – just as the moment of love is when you see its face again. It's that spark.

Being centred on the sun, the *rubedo* is hot, very hot, like the ruddy orange inside a kiln. It proceeds to what alchemists call the 'fourth degree' in this fourth and final main stage.

It is the antithesis of the *nigredo*. We are moving into the light now.

We are coming through.

Images of *rubedo* include the starry lion, as well as the red lion, the stars on his pelt immediately linking us to a larger context. We have also the *filius macrocosmi* (literally 'the son of the macrocosm', the greater world) who appears initially as a little cherubic Mercurius-child and who introduces further the idea that humanity is a microcosm that reflects the macrocosm of the Divine. We have the yolk of the egg that is like the sun, remembering the philosophic egg at the beginning. We have the Stone dyed red with pelican's blood that connects the Stone *to the heart* in terms of its qualities. We have innumerable golden coins as an image of spiritual (and literal) abundance; we have stones that represent the building blocks of life (like cells); we have a garden – sometimes a rose garden – of endless fertility, like a uterus; and we have 'the coffin of eternal life' which portrays and enacts the mystery of death and resurrection.

The *rubedo* is rich with imagery in the illustrations. There are also increasingly large images that include the alchemist's double or *Doppelgänger*, the androgyne of Sol and Luna in its final exalted form. We have landscapes, dreamscapes of lucid imagining that include the Heavenly City of Jerusalem and that build out increasingly to the sky, the sun, moon and stars – in fact out into the universe itself. We have cosmic structure then and what can only be described as sacred geometry.

Finally, through all of this, we have the *ouroboros* – the great snake with its tail in its mouth, signifying completion and an encircling – and we have the sun, permeating everything with its light.

mortificatio

So back to our story. We have left Sol and Luna standing together under Heaven with their glimpse of 'higher earth'. And now, another unexpected thing happens: they are eaten by the starry lion, who is also the green lion of *nigredo*. This is because their previous union has in some way to die, so we have separation again, but of a different kind – a separation that precedes a wedding where both of them, it seems, are strangely self-contained. Both of them are looking to the Source that goes beyond them. So there is a waiting, a clarifying, another kind of timing that is beyond the reach of desire.

In the flask the flames reverse, contracting round the philosophic egg, and with this, death comes in. It is another mortification, but it brings a key.

How are we to understand this? Alchemists say that the key to the Rose Garden, or Garden of Love, truly achieved, lies in this first phase. We think we're going up, and suddenly we're grounded, brought down, into a place that hurts, a place that perhaps we've forgotten. It is a soul place and maybe a soul wound – yet in *that*, alchemists say, lies the key and the 'rejected stone' that is the cornerstone of the whole building: 'Your heart is the wound and your heart is the key.' So this is a part we cannot leave out – or, if we try to, it is our soul that we end up leaving behind, and our greatest source of strength.

Literal death can come in here, too, together with images of old age and senescence that ground us into a recognition of mortality and compassion:

> *Twilight, over the graves.*
>
> *An old man bringing flowers.*[2]

There is a withdrawing of sexual energy and, as the heat begins to increase, Sol and Luna rise towards *Heaven*. This rising is the equivalent to a raising of awareness in preparation for love.

We leave them for the moment with that and turn now to birth in the flask, birth out of the egg itself. This is the birth (in embryo at first) of the *filius macrocosmi*, the philosopher's son who is also referred to as 'the child of the Work' and is the Stone, or final stone. This child, associated with Sol and Luna in quality and in terms of their development here, is also a seed of the cosmic man or transpersonal human being that the whole of this stage points to.

Meanwhile, the alchemist is worried. This is a critical moment, as any birth is. Is there too much heat? Is it too much too soon? The red colour is there – but it lacks something. It lacks full strength, faith, certainty, knowing. It lacks the spirit, the invisible descending. As one alchemist put it, continuing:

> For although God in the qualities of nature has become man, man in the qualities of nature has not yet become God or divine. The tincture of life still lacks the spirit of the Holy Ghost. In order that it may win this, it labours in itself towards fixation in the qualities of the sun.[3]

This is the labour now, in body and spirit, towards the birth of something that is real, durable and permanent within us, and that is good enough to make gold.

> For the sun gives spirit, colour, fixation and perfection to the tincture. The colour added to it by the sun is a crimson purple colour, a deep pomegranate red: this being the immutable and permanent colour.[4]

So what is born with this child? It is a universal or expanded quality of consciousness that is at the same time a threshold, like a membrane, a doorway we need to go through into a further dimension of our lives *so that the Spirit can enter in*.

As the *Janitor Pansophus* puts it:

> The eternal Father of all things, being not less wise in the ordering, than powerful in the creation of the world, has made the whole universe to cohere by means of secret influences and mutual subjection and obedience, things below being analogous to things above, and vice versa; so that both ends of the world are nevertheless united by a real bond of natural cohesion. Thus Hermes tells us that things below are the same as things above, and that things above are analogous to things below.[5]

Our relationship to the Divine appears at this point at the heart of the flask and the heart of the matter (the *materia*), really at the heart of the whole Work, we could say – its ruby heart. It introduces another vital realization: *that in this process we are also marrying ourselves, each one of us, alone*.

This is the birth of the Stone.

It introduces the two phases that follow. They are *multiplicatio* and *projectio*.

multiplicatio

Multiplicatio you will remember from *coagulatio*, under Mars. Here the idea is extended and amplified into a mastery of transmutation itself. In *coagulatio*, the work was yellowing, now it is a full reddening of the coagulated stone or tincture so that it has the potential for infinite multiplication beyond itself. It will not be capable of the next phase, the *projectio*, otherwise. Alchemists say that the Stone is not complete until it reaches this capacity – and in literal terms, is a test of the Stone's validity.

On a material level, we can understand *multiplicatio* here by analogy with publication. This book you are reading, which is one of thousands like it, was made as a result of the original page bromides with prepared artwork, 'multiplied' in the edition that it now exists in. The original typescript, written, worked on, revised and edited, in this sense is the Stone.

On a spiritual level we can understand it, for instance, as an active expression of the heart that multiplies and sustains itself through giving itself. In giving, it receives; expanding and strengthening reciprocally: love meeting love and in turn generating more love. Someone once asked Mother Theresa in Calcutta how she could do so much. Her reply was simple: 'Because I'm so in love.'

The temperature is raised to the highest here, so that the tincture can be perfected. The flames begin to fill the whole of the flask as it sheds its eerie and beautiful light. It is a body-heat, too, and a light you can sense or see, delineating us when we are alive with light and fire. We have a sharpness of focus around us then.

The fire makes the tincture, the redness, permanent. This brings us to a state of being that is strangely impervious to mood swings and other kinds of changes going on around us, whatever we are also going through on a human level. As we become less self-centred, less solely directed towards ourselves, we discover a fantastic source of energy in the heart.

This source of energy is revealed here, in this final act of coagulation, as the 'elixir' (the Elixir of Life). As another alchemical description puts it, suggestively:

In the human body there is concealed a certain substance of heavenly nature, known to very few, which needeth no medicament, being itself the incorruptible medicament ... It is a certain ethereal substance which preserves the other elemental parts of the body and causes them to continue ... In this fortress is the true and indubitable treasure, which is not eaten by moths, nor dug out by thieves, but remaineth for ever, and is taken hence after death.[6]

So now we are in a position to enter the Rose Garden, now we can understand Luna as Queen giving away her endless golden coins (*see figure*), now we can understand why Saturn waters the flowers there, holding the ground and the need for boundaries as he does. Now, too, we can begin to see the Stone as it emerges. The *Turba* describes its qualities:

The said one thing enters into every regimen and is found everywhere, being a stone and also not a stone; common and precious; hidden and concealed, yet known by everyone; of one name and many names ... This stone, therefore, is not a stone because it is more precious. Without it nature never operates anything. Its name is one, yet we have called it by many names on account of the excellence of its nature.[7]

'Regimen' here means process.

And where does the Stone get its energy from? It is said to feed in Mercurius.

The Stone we can see is both in us, as a part of us, and is *more than us* as it leads on to the next phase: *projectio*.

projectio

With *projectio* ('projection') we take another step. Now in a literal sense projection is what happens when the red tincture or 'powder' is applied: gold is magically multiplied. And as the *Philosophia reformata* has it:

> *Project on any body as much of it as you please, since its tincture shall be multiplied twofold. And if one part of it in the first place converts with its bodies a hundred parts: in the second it converts a thousand, in the third ten thousand, in the fourth a hundred thousand, in the fifth, a million, into the true sun-making and moon-making substance.*[8]

So in a literal sense we have projection *and then* multiplication, but here the two processes are placed *in reverse*.

Lapidis multiplicatiua Auri.

Projectio
- I.   1000
- II.   10000
- III. 100000
- IV.   1000000
- V.   10000000
- VI.   100000000
- VII. 1000000000
- VIII. 10000000000
- IX.   100000000000
- X.   1000000000000
- XI.   10000000000000
- XII. 100000000000000

Centum milliones millionum tingunt.

If you reverse the direction of multiplication, spreading and pro-liferating out, what you have is a movement upward and inward and back to the Source – to the head of the river. This reversal, like a salmon swimming upstream to leap, brings in the vertical dimension which crosses the horizontal line of multiplication. It is an extraordinary twist in the tale. Let's see what we can make of it all so far.

We have marriage here and we have death, and we have a place beyond death that alchemists see as a resurrection of the body *here* as well as *there*, on the other side. But to enter into this we have to go into the vertical, into ascension – we have to go in-wardly upstream to a place beyond time. This is the rising of spirit – like kundalini – in us that follows its descent. It is part of a single movement or circulation that brings spirit and soul to-gether, Heaven and Earth together – not just as two things that are related, but as *one*, one world, one kingdom.

So Sol and Luna meet. He is red, she is white. They have multi-plied, they have forged their hearts inwardly in themselves. So now as they meet, they are royal in heart, they are King and

Queen, they are ready – and not just because of themselves, as they realize, but by grace.

They stand together, as we may all stand one day: he in himself and she in herself. And as their eyes meet now, there is a clarity and a tenderness beyond anything they have known, although it is familiar too. They have known it all along.

And then they close their eyes.

And as the energy rises, this is where alchemy sees the resurrected body – the *corpus glorificatum*, the golden body of the man and the woman too, a body that can be identified with Christ transfigured, transformed through death. This body is, according to the alchemists themselves, 'transparent, clear as crystal, and with a fiery, rubeous hue'.[9] This corresponds to the full birth of the red tincture and it is here that, as the flask begins to blaze like the sun, we pass between worlds, experiencing the 'little death' (which was also the old euphemism for orgasm) which brings us to the birth of our spiritual selves.

Sol and Luna now move in their private act of wedding inside a church without walls. The 'Enigma of Bologna' in all its fluent beauty tells us something of how they may be feeling. She says to him:

> Aelia Laelia Crispis, *neither man nor woman, nor mongrel, nor maid, nor boy, nor crone, nor chaste, nor whore, nor virtuous, but all. Carried away neither by hunger, nor by sword, nor by poison, but by all. Neither in heaven, nor in earth, nor in water, but everywhere is her resting place.*

And he responds:

> Lucius Agatho Priscius, *neither husband, nor lover, nor kinsman, nor rejoicing, nor weeping, neither mound, nor pyramid, nor tomb, but all. He knows and knows not what he raised up to whom. This is a tomb that has no body in it. This is a body that has no tomb round it. But body and tomb are the same.*[10]

And now the alchemist raises the lid of a coffin containing himself – raised to life, purified in soul and spirit where soul and spirit are meeting and marrying. Now he sees – as we may – that there is death and there is no death. And he gives birth to himself as the Red King, the king that Sol has been all this time in the making.

Meanwhile Sol and Luna rest as they move, suspended, blending in the heaven and joy of each other that is their resurrection so that we can also see that:

> *Death is the wedding,*
> *Love is the wedding.*

They bring us to the same place.

Now there is integration, true wholeness. The longer the marrying goes on, the more awesome it becomes. As Sol and Luna, who from a Christian viewpoint can be identified with Christ and Mary, enter into what has been called the Theogamy or sacred marriage, 'theogamy' meaning 'married to God' or 'in God', so, as alchemists say, 'God becomes man'. Soul unites with spirit so we become *all* that we are. The body is completely spiritualized and capable of spiritual embodiment. 'The fixed rules over the volatile' – this is a reality that is unbreakable.

What are the effects of this full raising of consciousness? At this point the alchemist begins to discover some unusual abilities. As the *Book of the Holy Trinity* has it:

When a man holds the red stone in his hand he becomes invisible. When, in order to warm him, one binds the stone with a kerchief to his body, he rises into the air and travels wherever he wishes. If he wants to go down to earth again, he removes the stone from his body and lands softly.[11]

This is clearly levitation – or, as we might also say, an ability to move between the worlds, between different levels, at will. There is also clairvoyance, clairaudience, telepathic communication, precognition, guidance or channelling, distant healing, healing 'miracles', and the work of deliverance that is crudely called exorcism ... to name only some of them.

These are magical abilities, but in alchemy they only really come at the point at which we are equipped to handle them. They are gifts that come out of purity, not toys to play manipulative games with. No true alchemist would sanction misuse of them for one minute.

These are the effects of the Stone.

And Sol and Luna? At the hour of conjunction (supposedly in Pisces) they are said to transcend all opposition. 'Quicksilver takes sulphur into itself, and vice versa. Both forces die as foes and lovers,' one text reads.[12] In another image sun and moon mutually eclipse each other so that he is only aware of *her* face and not his own, as she is of his. And in this union of love and dying, and through it – as improbable as it may seem to be – *she begins to become man*, and *he begins to become woman*, even as he remains outwardly a 'man' and she a 'woman'. This is their transformation and their androgyny, as sun and moon blend and circulate, alternating between them like a current in a figure of eight that is eternity. He is now referred to as 'the man of paradise' and she

is henceforth a most substantial seraphic angel, she can make herself doctor, theologian, astrologer, divine magician, she can make herself whatsoever she will, and do and have whatsoever she will: for all qualities have but one will in agreement and harmony. And this same one will is God's eternal infallible will; and from henceforth the divine man is in his own nature become one with God.[13]

This is the wedding that their candles celebrate (*see figure*), and they are exalted here together in their royal and naked equality – pictured standing with the globe between them, sun above him, moon above her, surrounded by a ring of golden stars, in the space of the cosmic circle that points, like the *ouroboros*, towards the end of the Work.

Two jet trails cross, streaking the sky like a sign …

From here on, the wedding and the alchemist's perceptions fully enter into a cosmic and transcending dimension that is union and unity, where all paradoxes are blended. It is a place of liberation as well as recognition that Daskalos has called ABSOLUTE BEINGNESS (referring to God)[14] and that the *Tibetan Book of the Dead* calls 'the Clear Light of the Void'. It is both: depending on how we see it, when we see it. This is where the *rubedo* takes us: into circles of wholeness that ripple out from the Stone – far out into the sea of our furthest understanding where the Above – as alchemy sees it – reveals the secret, substance and essence (or quintessence) of what is Below: inside us, around us, and finally at the heart and centre of our lives lit by the sun.

This is the Philosopher's Stone. So here is another exercise, the first of three in this final stage, to give you space for your own consciousness and its expansion.

You might want to do this with some music that suits your mood and that helps you to relax your mental activity.

Take a moment to sit quietly, then slowly bring your awareness up to a point about 18 inches (45 cm) above your head. You will experience it as a point, possibly like a star.

When you feel a link there, just reflect on your relationship to the Above. How connected do you feel to it? How do you see it or sense it?

Then bring your awareness slowly down around the outside edges of your body until it reaches between your feet and under the floor or ground to the same distance below (there is an equivalent point here which is referred to as the magnetic point – or sometimes as the earth chakra).[15]

Reflect on your connection to the Below, at the depth, and horizontally either side of you and around you. Again, see what comes.

Then see how connected these two places are for you. How could they be more so?

Come back when you're ready, feeling your feet on the ground, and again, make some notes on your experience of Above and Below, and where they connect for you, including any images and insights you may have had.

What does their connection mean for you?

CIRCLES OF WHOLENESS

Circles of wholeness ripple out from the Stone. The first rippling circle is contained in the phrase: 'The sun and its shadow complete the work.' This is what alchemists call the *umbra solis*, meaning the shadow of the sun.

The sun is pictured shining down on the globe of the earth with the moon, and the shadow of the sun that the earth casts, falling behind it. The ring of stars surrounding it is the Chymical Wedding or Heavenly Marriage.

The earth here is revealed as the Stone. The sun's shadow is the earth's and the moon's – and the tincture, or Stone, they say, is composed of both. In other words, *it is both light and shadow*. It couldn't be substance, it couldn't be material or incarnate otherwise. It couldn't be made.

The process of the Work, as we have seen, includes both light and shadow at every stage. Privation and pain go alongside expansion and joy. This is not only true to our experience, but also introduces something more profound. We are not only made up of light and shadow, but – as alchemy says – we cannot transmute and embody our light *without* our shadow. In embracing it lies the gift of being uniquely human.

So we need our dross as well as our gold, because it is out of the dross that the gold comes: it is the blackness with the light that creates it and makes it *not just light, but gold*.

☿

The second ripple, which concerns Sol and Luna at the end, is described by the phrase 'the squaring of the circle' (*see figure*). The motto from the *Rosarium* reads: 'Make a circle out of a man and woman, derive from it a square, and from the square a triangle: make a circle and you will have the Philosopher's Stone.'[16] Again, it reads like a riddle but actually it is quite clear. The triangle

Here followeth the Figure conteyning all
the secrets of the Treatife both great & small

above the couple, linking to the 'third point' or apex above them, signifies the unity of body, soul and spirit that the wedding represents. The square inside the triangle represents the synthesis of the four elements: fire, earth, air and water, all of which have been used in the process. (The number 4 is also a number of wholeness: four corners, the four directions, etc.) The circle around the whole thing signifies 'the stone's transformation into permanent redness', as a result of which woman turns into man and man into woman. This means that not only does the stone create this ultimate and radical blending, *but that Sol and Luna also make the stone*. Without a man and a woman, in other words, there would be no stone.

That is what we can make here by coming together, if we can understand the process and what it also requires – which is that we also marry ourselves, that we become 'one' to ourselves, both as a woman and as a man. We can only accomplish this by understanding that we both contain 'the other' within ourselves – not only in terms of *anima* and *animus* but literally in a relationship. You are in me as I am in you. You are in my heart as I am in yours. But only when we know that that we can each be strong enough, 'stony' enough, to be free and not impede the other's progress.

And what is made between us, through love? Through making love? Wholeness, again. We can see it in the diagram below in terms of how a man and a woman connect with each other and aspire to one another:

FEMININE – feminine spirit   masculine spirit – MASCULINE
masculine soul   feminine soul

Out of these two comes the androgyne, that also involves the recognition that we each have unique gender, whether as heterosexuals, bisexuals, lesbians or gays. The androgyne is not a stereotype. In reality, it is each of us, unique as we are.

Sally Potter's lyric, sung by Jimmy Somerville in an extraordinary soprano at the end of her film *Orlando*, summarizes this beautifully:

> *I am coming, I am coming*
> *Here I am –*
> *Neither a woman or a man*
>
> *We are joined, we are one*
> *With the human race*
> *We are joined, we are one*
> *With the human face ...*[18]

The third ripple is brief. It involves the fifth element or quintessence which is revealed as a synonym for the etheric or subtle body. This gives us access to this expanded realm of feeling and sensing – both inside and outside ourselves. It is our innate sensitivity which is alchemized into being: darkened, lightened, purged, purified and refined until it really becomes our own, with all we can then achieve with it. It returns us to Heaven, and Earth, and each other in a new way. It feeds on care and, like the alchemical process itself, on honesty as well as stillness, Nature, movement and meditation. It is the free inner body of who we are. It wants to breathe. And it wants to be.

The fourth ripple evokes this quality of feeling that is purified (like the stone) through emotion, and specifically two qualities that come in in this last stage: detachment and objectivity.

These are a feature of out-of-body and near-death experience, when what we are used to clinging on to ceases to concern us in the same way. They are qualities we can have *here* too. They are born out of expanded awareness – an awareness that sees beyond narcissistic self-preoccupation and that recognizes we are on a planet that is in need.

And in relationship to each other? Jung puts is challengingly and in a way that points to the heart of the *rubedo*:

> *Emotional relationships are relationships of desire, tainted by coercion and constraint; something is expected from the other person, and that makes him and ourselves unfree. Objective cognition lies hidden behind the attraction of the emotional relationship; it seems to be the central secret. Only through objective cognition is the real* coniunctio *possible.*[18]

We may then come on to realize, as a result of this, that the wedding is not just two of us, it is *all of us*.

The fifth ripple concerns the Christ of alchemy who as it happens is rather different from the Christ in many churches. He is both closer and more resurrected, more personal, challenging and radical. Alchemists see him as the personification of the Red King or 'rose man' (the lover), as well as the *corpus glorificatum*, the golden or glorified body given by grace that the *rubedo* opens us towards. For an alchemist, Christ has been here and has done the work already – so he guides and leads us on to this accomplishment inside each of us. 'I am the Resurrection and the Life,' as he said. Christian or not, we can see the significance of this here and Christians can come to appreciate him in a new way, entering as he does into our shadow as well as our light, concerned above all with our truth and wholeness. And then in the Eucharist we can see him as alchemy sees him: giving the red substance of himself in the bread and the wine, as soul and spirit, matter and spirit, combined, offering us the sacrament of unity.

So Christ here is the Beloved Master, brother, friend and un-conditional lover in the words of his last, new, commandment: '... that you love one another as I have loved you ...' (at the Last Supper, in the Gospel of John).

The sixth ripple brings us to the close of the Work itself, into the realm of silence that the alchemist and his *soror mystica* (in this case) gesture to at the end of the *Mutus liber* (the Silent Book). That is both the secret they have found and the limit of what they can say.[19] This takes us back to the very beginning, where in order to feel something, or to allow something to clarify or emerge, silence is necessary (*see p.3*). Silence is part of the work and essential to our containment, our flask. Silence and speech are reciprocal: speech that comes out of an inner silence is very different from speech that knows no silence. Silence leaves us open to pure experience. Silence means we can listen and be guided. Silence means we also have space in us to receive what we don't yet know. We all need this.

The seventh and last ripple is the alchemist as man or woman. The co-worker, as *soror mystica* 'lover for the work' is shown ex-alted in her own purity as 'Queen of Heaven' and as part of Sophia, where in one text she says:

> I am the end and my beloved is the beginning. I am the whole work and all science is hidden in me.[20]

His task, and all of ours, is to become 'cosmic man' in a full in-dwelling of the Self that is both old man and child: both wisdom and care, simplicity and openness at the same time. He is shown – sometimes like Atlas – in touch with 'All That There Is', stretched, enlarged to his full potential, taking on his responsibility as a co-creator as part of the cause and effect of Creation. And in one text that stretches our ordinary credibility, it is said:

> *The work is not brought to perfection unless it ends in the simple ... for man is the most worthy of living things and nearest to the simple, and this because of his intelligence.*[21]

And as T. S. Eliot said too, some centuries later, writing four or five years after Yeats' death, in 'Little Gidding':

> *Quick, now, here, always*
> *A condition of complete simplicity*
> *(Costing not less than everything)*
> *And all shall be well*
> *All manner of things shall be well*
> *When the tongues of flame are in-folded*
> *Into the crowned knot of fire*
> *And the fire and the rose are one.*[22]

And the great snake, the *ouroboros*, pauses with its tail in its mouth, not only as an expression of closure and roundness, but also – perhaps – of the unified field of matter and mind, and the cosmic destiny that is also ours. 'Oneness.'

Here is a second exercise, so you can explore the wedding in yourself.

Again sitting comfortably, take a moment to close your eyes and feel your breathing – and also how your body is feeling.

See if you can briefly visualize the colour red and the colour white (or white and then red, as appropriate), being aware of how you feel about these colours. If you can't actually see the colours, don't worry – you will still be bringing their energy to mind.

How do you see these colours side by side? How do they relate for you?

Leaving the colours aside, just take a moment to connect to the fact that there is a man and a woman, or a woman and a man, in you.

Give yourself time to experience one and then the other by bringing your attention to each of them in turn.

How do you experience them? Where are they in you? What do they look like? See if you can allow an image of each of them to emerge.

Then see if you can get a sense of how they relate to each other from their respective places. What do they think of each other? Is there anything they'd like to say to each other?

Can you visualize a place they'd like to meet? You might like to ask one of them to point to the place within you. See what the place is like.

Then see if you can picture them both there together, standing together. What happens when they do?

Be aware of what is happening to you.

How do you feel towards them?

Is there anything they have to give you now – either in a phrase, a symbolic object or a gesture? Can you see what it means to accept their gifts?

Ask each of them what they need from you in return, so you can really accept and receive what they have to give.

Now just take a moment to say anything you'd like to say to them.

Then leave them where they are.

Bring your awareness to your heart to rest there in silence, before you come back to make your notes or drawings.

This is an exercise you can always repeat, with or without the two colours at the beginning. The same applies to the other exercises in this book. The important thing is that you use them. Always remember, though, to take them slowly, so you can allow what is actually trying to happen to take place. If you rush them, you will get far less. Your psyche is not a machine, it is a sensitive instrument with its own timing – just like the process itself. As Shakespeare said, 'The ripeness is all.'

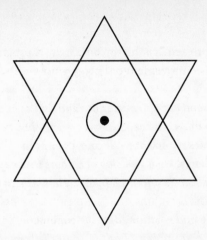

The *rubedo* is vast – and if it isn't the longest of the stages, it is certainly the largest, in conception and actuality. It is not only large in itself, but also in many ways it incorporates all of the stages of the Lesser and Greater Work within itself. So in the opening *mortificatio* we have a *nigredo*; with Sol and Luna's ascension and sublimation we have another *solutio*; in the phase of *multiplicatio* where the stone is 'tested' we have a *coagulatio*, before the *projectio* and all its consequences – its ripples – take us into the essence of the *rubedo* itself, into the heart of the matter that is simultaneously Above and Below.

At the heart of the *rubedo* (and in its 'mind', too[23]) there is paradox and a movement beyond paradox – finally into the unity of life and death itself. We cannot reach the whole of it here: it is a lifetime's work, perhaps the work of many lives. But it offers us a structure and (in Anne Bancroft's phrase) 'a map of hidden treasure'.[24] Look at the 'ruby thread', the royal thread of the heart running through your life, and ask yourself how true to it you are being ... considering too what it means to marry yourself; because the real point of this crowning stage lies in a reclaiming of the nobility of our original nature – our *royal* nature.

Mercurius is present, visibly or not, right through the process – there could be no movement or energy without him. As Jung says:

> *Mercurius stands at the beginning and end of the work: he is the* prima materia, *the* caput corvi *(raven's head), the* nigredo; *as dragon he devours himself and as dragon he dies, to rise again as the* lapis. *He is the play of colours in the* cauda pavonis *and the division into four elements. He is the hermaphrodite that was in the beginning, that splits into the classical brother-sister duality and is reunited in the* coniunctio, *to appear once again at the end in the radiant form of the* lumen novum, *the stone. He is metallic yet liquid, matter yet spirit, cold yet fiery, poison and yet healing draught – a symbol uniting all opposites.*[25]

So in one sense he is everything, all of it – but perhaps *ever-present* would be more exact. As Jung is also quoted as saying in the film about his own life, *A Matter of Heart*: 'The great danger of consciousness is that it is one-sided ...'[26] and here we can get closer, I believe, to who this being is. *Through* him every level is simultaneously present: all these things can be together at the same time. We can even see him in the word 'hermaphrodite' as a compound of Hermes and Aphrodite, the goddess of love.

Behind him, in Greek myth, stands Hermes himself – the Hermes before Hermes Trismegistos, who is the god of travellers, trade and eloquence. He is a messenger with a winged helmet and winged sandles, and he can move fast. He is also a trickster, a shape-shifter, in the story where he steals Apollo's cattle and then finally charms him into submission by playing the lyre. As an infant prodigy he becomes one of the most popular gods, always sunny and helpful, solving apparently intractable problems. He is quick, light and shadowy all at once. He has many different children by many different kinds of women, not least the great god Pan.

His Roman name matures into Mercury, from which we finally have Mercurius and the adjective 'mercurial'. Here he is associated particularly with money and the energy that it represents. He is *quicksilver*, if you like, then (Mercurius probably would).

In alchemy, he matures still further, appearing, like Asclepius (the god of healing before him), holding the staff of healing – the *caduceus* with its entwined snakes (*see illustration on p.66*). So for alchemists he is a healer, too: he is the prime mover of psychic healing, and wholeness as a result. And it's here that he takes on more serious qualities without losing any of his innate and rule-bending gifts.

So what is his energy – and why is he so vital for us?

Mercurius is fluid, like water running over a mirror: he is elastic, playful, flexible, sexual – and as a dissolving agent (a dissolver or solver of problems) he is the fluid, the juice that dissolves our blockages, revealing them as self-imposed limitations created by fear. He is the lust we can discover is a lust for life itself: he is the urge towards every spontaneous and uninhibited gesture; and his genius (and joyfulness) is that he never loses his sense of humour, black as it may be at times. In all of this *he is our unconscious* – the unconscious that underpins and flows under everything, and here he appears too as a guiding thread in our dreams that are always messages from a greater reality.

And part of his flexibility is that he remains indefinable: he cannot be made to mean any one thing alone, and his gift of healing may, in the way it happens, seem like poison or even destruction, especially when one way of life for us is over.

Whatever we are, he will appear as its opposite: if we're too light, he will appear as dark; if we are too sexual, he will come as sensuality; if we are too sedentary, he will want exercise. He goes for the gap. As Patrick Harpur, who celebrates him through Eileen in *Mercurius*, remarks:

In fact, it is not we who know Mercurius but he who knows himself through us and in us. We participate in his knowledge of himself. We only know Creation by participating in the process of Creation.[27]

If his call is to the physical, to life, it is not a heavy quality of physicality he represents: in the Work, *he keeps the stone soft*, so it doesn't become hard and rigid. However individualized we may become, Mercurius will never allow us to turn to stone – or not for long.

In all of this I have been using the male pronoun. But of course Mercurius is more than that – and as 'the androgynous one' he lives in both sexes, and often more easily in a woman. For Sol and Luna too, Mercurius is an essential magic between them – teasing, laughing, forgiving and healing. A male and female Mercurius can have a lot of fun together.

But to come full circle, there is energy here even greater than Mercurius – and that is the sun. If Saturn accompanies Mercurius as his own shadow, it is the sun who finally centres him in the *punctum solis* in which his symbol or signature appears, at the centre:

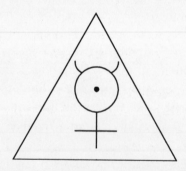

And it is there, and then, through all his journey that he becomes light, too: gold that is alive with life within us.

So I'd like to suggest an exercise here for you to open further to this quality for yourself.

Sitting, or lying, as you wish, take a moment to just feel your body and all its humming streams of energy.

Be aware of the fluid in your body – all its juices.

Now see if you can connect to the idea of a positive shadow in you – a positive part of you that may be 'other' than who you think you are and that needs to come to light.

See if you can feel it in your body. Does any image of it want to come forward? If you feel any tension or resistance here, breathe into your body, relax and allow what is trying to emerge.

See if you can feel this in your heart-area too ... and then ... it in your mind.

Notice what comes.

Then reconnect to this quality in your body, feeling and allowing its energy. See if you can allow a gesture to emerge naturally and spontaneously that expresses it. It may be sitting, standing or kneeling, stretching or moving. See what wants to come, in spite of any self-consciousness.

See what this gesture is trying to show you – and then reflect on how much space you are giving this quality in your life.

This is your Mercurius. How healthy or unhealthy is s/he? And how imprisoned? How contained? Where might the balance be? Remember that in the shadow, all 'monsters' are monsters of our own neglect and, as Freud said, to emphasize an idea of importance we may first need to over-exaggerate it. In other words, it may appear temporarily in a heightened form because its expression has been suppressed.

☿

So what are the implications of all of this? Where do the *rubedo* and the end of the Work bring us to? They open us finally to life – to our lives – and to the embodiment of spirit. This is a reality – it has happened to people and it will go on happening. As Mother Meera put it in her little book, *Answers:*

> Q: *Why is devotion to the Divine important?*
> MM: *If you have devotion you will get everything.*[28]

It is not as out of reach as it may seem.

As a friend, the poet Rosemary Palmeira, suddenly remarked in conversation as we were standing to leave, 'By the way, the colour of heaven is red – not orange, not yellow, but warm red.' She had seen it for herself, with her eyes and her heart, inside.

What *rubedo* requires is a detachment then, and at the same time a deeper participation, a more personal involvement, in the Self. At this point, alchemists say, the stone is strong enough in the flask to withstand its seal being broken. There is something permanent here now.

Yet of course, to the extent it may still be lacking in something, we get drawn back into the process, guided infallibly by the truth of where we actually are. I can say this from my own experience. The *rubedo* we think we're in may turn out to be a *solutio* that requires further coagulation before it can be made real again. And so the wheel turns.

One of the acid tests of *rubedo* is that in it, spirit and matter become of equal importance. We can turn from metaphysical discussion to needing to fix a loose screw in the oven, for instance.

In *rubedo* we are led by the spirit, guided by it, even obedient to it speaking through all of life. After all, it is all there is.

Marrying oneself is another test of *rubedo* and in that 'coming in to ourselves' we can experience perhaps most directly the peculiar difficulty of making the stone. We can feel all the ache of it inside our skin. In *rubedo*, we live alone in so far as we live *with* or *in* ourselves – whatever our actual living arrangement may be – from the flask that becomes the centre, the stone that we go out from and return to. As Ted Hughes once put it, simply and honestly, 'One does get to know oneself, after all.' [29]

At the same time we live for the Self here, however we experience it. So as another female participant said during a workshop, 'My life is no longer simply my own'. She also spoke of 'getting myself out of the way'. This relates to what we commit ourselves to doing with our lives here.

In *rubedo* the emphasis shifts upwards to the heart from the solar plexus, so the sexual act itself is transformed in its intention. The wedding is beyond sexuality, or beyond sex as the primary motivating force. Sex becomes a conductor for a far greater energy, just as it is in the practice of tantra. It actually allows much *more* feeling, so our sexuality is both released and enlarged, in love as well as friendship, in a companionship of openness and respect. As June Singer remarks, in emphasizing the humanness here:

> Without a sense of disjunction, the person will become at once tender and firm, flexible and strong, ambiguous and precise, focussed in thinking and diffused in awareness, nurturing and guiding, giving and receiving. It will be like listening to a duet skilfully played by a pianist and a violinist, when one does not hear the two separate instruments so much as the harmonious interplay between them.[30]

So it becomes like music, which is the language of feeling. It becomes beauty.

And there is more here too, because this level of awareness opens the door on an expanded loving that goes beyond the bourgeois construct of 'coupledom' and its self-enclosed exclusivity that is the shadow of *solutio*. Here we see that the real romanticism of love involves all of us – especially now – and the *rubedo* suggest a new paradigm whose time has come. We are invited on to new ground here, to where – as already mentioned – the wedding is all of us, and where our partnerships will both demand

and create much more out of us in this crucible of new fire. As we grow in our individuality, love itself becomes our guidance, our expression and our restraint.

The love we have and share is given to us as part of a greater love: a Great Love that is the love of God in action. And action brings us back to earth. As close as we get to Heaven, we need earth too, always. There is a famous Zen proverb that reads:

Before enlightenment, chopping wood and carrying water.
After enlightenment, chopping wood and carrying water.

And at the end of *The Chymical Wedding of Christian Rozencreutz*, after all he has been through, Christian becomes a porter – a guardian of one of the gates at the request of the king.

So *rubedo* leads us towards commitment and service – doing whatever we do on behalf of others, not merely ourselves. As Leo Marks put it memorably in his 'Code Poem for the French Resistance':

The life that I have is all that I have,
And the life that I have is yours[31]

Beyond ego here, there is a quality of passionate humility and even anonymity. It doesn't matter who I am, what matters is what is being done. So in *rubedo* we can transcend our own process, even as we remain in a personal process for as long as we live. We can be close, in this sense, to everyone saluting the gold in them as well as living the gold in ourselves.

The equivalent of this in Buddhism is the Bodhisattva Vow, in which the enlightened person chooses not to leave the wheel of death and rebirth until everyone has come to their inner light, their sun. And *rubedo* finally means *both* worlds here: Earth because of Heaven, and Heaven because of Earth, bridged into one continuous world where the barriers come down, the doors of perception are cleansed, horizontal and vertical meet, and we begin to see into the heart of the rose.

The One Coming Closer

Who is this who is constantly coming closer?
It is the man in the ship's hold.
It is what the body knows, what it holds.

And this one who is constantly coming closer,
Ah, that is the spontaneous, mercurial one,
Imprisoned in the cedar root on the mustard seed.

He is no-one we know; he is not Jehovah,
Or an obedient ermine-caparisoned king.
He is one nearer than near, closer than fingernails.

Are we all then religious? It must be so.
We know him, we see him, we hold him every day.

He is the one constantly coming closer.

ROBERT BLY

EIGHT

ROSA MUNDI

It is the glory of God to conceal a thing;
But the honour of kings is to search out a matter.
The heaven for height, and the earth for depth,
And the heart of kings is unsearchable.
Take away the dross from the silver,
And there shall come forth a vessel for the finer

PROVERBS 25:2–4

Even as the pristine Wisdom now reveals its presence in all the forces of Nature, in all the sense-perceptible outer world upon Earth, so in the future will Love be revealed – Love as a new force of Nature, living in all the phenomena which man will have around him. This is the secret of all future evolution.

RUDOLF STEINER, OCCULT SCIENCE

But now it is. IS,
Amen.

RAINER MARIA RILKE
(AFTER FINISHING THE DUINO ELEGIES)

We are not the message ... we are the messengers ... the message is love.

WIM WENDERS, IN THE FILM FAR AWAY, SO CLOSE

ROSA MUNDI

One world, one kingdom.

When a rose in the chest of every man and woman flowers, then we shall see as we did in the beginning. We shall touch and feel, taste and savour, smell and linger, and hear the soul of sound. We will remember that we were all feeling, and are, and we will see how we have been this down the length of centuries. We will see inwardly in blood that is light – rose-blood – and we will know the secret lines of light between all of us that span cities, seas and continents.

We will see how we've been every kind of rose, and had to be: love rose, loving; desert rose, in the unknown; death rose, grieving; nothing rose, with nothing to show – and in each new rose, intact in its bud, stirring in its sap, we will know that love is working behind everything. Love, in every particle. Love.

And who are we then as we cram smiling into any living picture? We are a Rose Garden.

Do you remember how in Heaven you saw us standing in a flower, and all its petals were our faces raying white soft flame? And how there was no marrying or giving in marriage, and yet we were all together and our love was for the One?

It was no dream, it was our future selves you were seeing, as far away as they seem, through all this living and dying: on a journey that means only we become more ourselves, where our hearts can grow more like the Heart of It All.

Because only the heart can see who we are: only the heart can know the true gold.

Rosa. Rose. Be open now –

And we will see how we are a tribe and a company, in circle after circle rippling out and intersecting. We will see how we are all entering each other – as gifts to each other, mirroring and completing each other: and how we are all unique angles on the centre. And we will see as we move and speak in the silence of sharing and touch how it is only in interweaving that we make the Rose. And all our binding of each other will die, as our jealousy will have to die. The snake in our eyes will die, as the eagle awakens. And we will know how all the hurt and aching was only for this – that we come to live in God in one another's hearts.

And it is here the New Loving begins; the love we have known, the love that is real.

Rose in its dew-like wine scent – can you sense, can you breathe it in, now?

Red. White. Red. Gold.

In love there is a fire, and in the fire there is a flame. And in the flame there is another who has known us before time. He knows her now, she knows his name. And it's in the face behind our faces, the voice inside our voices, where light gathers at our edges as our eyes meet again.

And she can stretch him to the edges of his life. And he can take her into the depth of her fire.

And who are they? The ones who have agreed to love, to open each other to the quick and the core of their being.

And so his eyes can see her as she is, and her hands can know him as he is. And the seeing and the knowing is in them and beyond them like a star. They are following a dancing flame into the darkness that is daylight, reading the signs inside out and learning to trust. Because what they live is in matter, but it is light. It is light; but not even their love can fathom it. And it moves, as it breathes, with its own life.

So she is one and many, as she is woven in herself, one and many as we all are dancing together; one by one for the journey that is love, lover by lover that is stardust, flesh-grass and stone.

We are all lovers in the Rose.

And this is the miracle of red and white, and where they blend ... in the smoky pink-veined quartz of this crystal: this other body that they make as they love, this body that they leave and return to as it grows

silently in the in-between space of them

in the rose that is the crux
                    of Heaven and Earth
                              as they stand:

Where upwards through the skein of the air like a warmth, the messengers with their outstretched hands and arms are waiting, as agile as the birds have always told us. And you can feel them in the standing light behind your eyes, brushing and pulsating through the edges of your skin: where they and the awakened dead and we and the living dead are one as the screen of our senses begins to rise:

And see down into this flask of precious earth, among its streams
of cloud and coastline edge twisting like a kaleidoscope

    of day-glow rainbow colours under the dome of the sky

– see down among the supermarket trolleys and queuing cars;
faces walking, homeward and homeless, sighing, dreaming,
shouting and parting ... earth that is gleaming green, littered and
scarred ... harvest fields of gold and dustbowls that are starving
... party balloons like kites and war-torn city wire ... dolphins
that leap and species that are dying ... nights that are moonlit
and nights that are red ... promises made and blown like glass ...
clenched cries of love and cries of tortured pain

bubbling, fermenting, congealing
                          crucified and rising

to fall in the mercy of rain

And see, as your heart wonders *oh when*, how all this has to be
before it can be – before we can feel, before we can choose the
heart's way, choose life again

and walk as we walk here in feeling, seeing how deeply this earth
                                    reveals us
                                        rising

Blue rose
              Rose of the Winds
Rose window
             rose-wisdom
                Rosarium

– in this narrowing through the gate to where your heart is free –
where it is finding your face with no mirror but feeling – *where
all this time secretly a rose has been opening in you* .

Where the key comes, unexpectedly given; as the banked shingle gleams where the waves foam white and the sun slants out as you hear a voice saying, 'Give yourself eternally to this, into each moment of its passing – in each moment is the life you will always or never live ...'

– give, and the rose opens; receive, and the rose is beautiful, is unashamed of its beauty and is here and now as the birds are and the breeze is, and It Is

Rosehip red and hawthorn blood-red

   Blackthorn white and pale pink, Peace white

And this clear light rose of no name you are choosing

And it is: a step in aloneness, all-oneness

      into the heart of the circle that is the centre

         where every layer is stripped like an onion

           till only your heart of hearts is left:

And it is
when you taste a taste like wine in your mouth

And it is
where your searing voice soars in its swan-throated song

And it is
      in the sound of galloping hooves
And it is in the man and woman making love with you

And it is as we pray in the inner of who we are – it is when we remember to praise and say it out loud – and it is in the way our minds are being changed
      now

And it is in the brightness of your face like a sun

And it is when we see that 'It is all love – all of it'

And it is
as we see what a clear lucid dream we are being held in

in awe – across the woven fields of mist, lights and crimson sky
– at the design

And it is this rose of light

And it is as the membrane begins to stretch

It is where the village shines like a jewel in the freezing air

And it is in the letter you tear to open

It is as its wrapped red bud and stem lances the last veil, barrier,
bandage left

Where you feel the bell in your heart like a tongue, beating

'Open your arms and stand as you are'

And it is a Rose Song of Songs then, as it bursts, it breaks, it
flows through in calm, surrender, balm:

It is the music of the spheres of the heart ringing and answering,
feeling for feeling, pealing out

It is a great rose of light fanned, spreading and covering everything

– as we pass through into the centre of the circle

that is formless light, breathing between us

shaped as we are in each contour of our skin

in all our breathing-feeling-being become the same

one body

in You

Lord of Love

at the apex

where You are in us and as us

in this communion as we embrace

As it turns and turns and turns round

Above and below, all blended beyond imagining

And then it goes beyond all words, it goes beyond sound ...
it goes into the place where Love is loving through us

And it is the crown

given over our heads, rooted deep in our dreaming flesh

One world, one kingdom

World without end

Where we go into the light of our being

NINE

ENDING

'Is that the one thing I still needed to know?'

'No,' the alchemist answered. 'What you still need to know is this: before a dream is realized, the Soul of the World tests everything that was learned along the way. It does this not because it is evil, but so that we can, in addition to realizing our dreams, master the lessons we've learned as we've moved towards that dream. That's the point at which most people give up. It's the point at which, as we say in the language of the desert, one 'dies of thirst just when the palm trees have appeared on the horizon'.

'Every search begins with beginner's luck. And every search ends with the victor's being severely tested.'

The boy remembered an old proverb from his country. It said that the darkest hour of the night came just before the dawn.

PAULO COELHO, THE ALCHEMIST

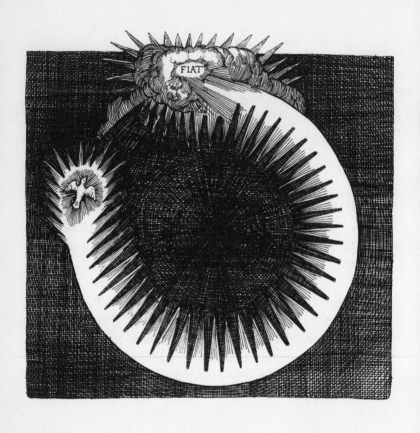

SUMMA

Strait is the gate to the holy place
– its keyhole is in the heart's door.

As a way of concluding, it seems useful to map the whole of the journey that forms the *Magnum Opus* or Great Work that we have passed through, with all the experience and insight it has hopefully evoked and illuminated for you.

As contemporary astrologer and psychotherapist Liz Greene points out, we can also understand the process as being like a spiral in which each time we find ourselves going 'back into something' (as we say) or each time some aspect that these stages and phases represent 'comes round again', a little more of the Stone is formed. So it is a process we can repeat with greater clarity each time. And, as she adds:

> ... and once there is even a tiny piece of it, one does not suffer in the same way. Perhaps one does not have to suffer at all, in the sense we usually think of it, because there is a constant co-operation with what is happening, and it feels like more of a choice. But yes, I think we meet the same characters in our individual myths, and undergo the same characteristic experiences which are our greatest spurs to growth.[1]

We can see it like this, then, remembering the circular diagram of the planets that alchemists alluded to (*see p.20*), with Saturn as the outermost ring and the sun at the centre:

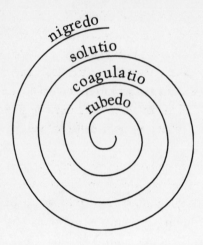

So while the process is linear as a structure and in terms of a sequential approach on our part, in the actual dimension of our lives, it is not. As Carole Bruce pointed out from her own experience of illness, 'I was being broken down, washed and grounded at the same time.'[2]

So we can also understand the process as multi-dimensional – like a hologram – because of the way we live at all the different levels of our being simultaneously. Life itself is never static either, as we know all too well: change is always with us and as the wheel turns we can find ourselves going through parts of the Work again and again as we need to. And we may need to without necessarily *wanting* to, or being aware that it is precisely what we do need. At the same time what we can call our 'Higher Self' generally *does* know and this specifically comes to the fore at the end of the process in an increasingly real and practical way: our Higher Selves here are embodied as the Stone and are a part of its function. So when we reach beyond our ordinary minds in this way, we are using the Stone. And we can use it daily, recognizing that guidance is always beyond the emotional plane, and the swings and pushes of our immediate desires.

Patience, again. And prayer, as any alchemist knows. Always that.

Can we lose what we have gained? On one level, no. As Bob Moore has also said, our experiences never forget us.[3] But we can lose touch with them and it is here we need to recognize that we are beings in need of constant self-maintenance, whatever that may require. There is no sitting on our laurels here; in fact there are no laurels in alchemy, or in any developed spiritual understanding either – there is only self-renewal, as every season knows.

And *who* we are – who you and I are, in the end – remains a mystery too, however well we may know ourselves at a human level. As Oscar Wilde remarked with his usual freshness, a century ago now:

> *The final mystery is oneself. When one has weighed the sun in the balance, and measured the steps of the moon, and mapped out the seven heavens star by star, there still remains oneself. Who can calculate the orbit of his own soul?*[4]

Even in our age of therapy and self-examination, that remains true. We may discover, too, that what is permanent within us is not ours for the keeping and that it only works in being used or given. Who we are is what we belong to. And beyond that, there is a silence in all of us that is ineffable – a silence in which, however we understand it, we are also in God.

And if one day we know, we will find that we also lived because we didn't. And so the gesture of the secret remains, just as the open gesture of the Work remains. It is there for us to do, and the path lies in living it.

A chart follows of steps we have made. Having scanned it and seen it whole, you might want to evaluate your journey as a whole, this time around, bearing in mind that you can refer to it at any time in the future as well. You might also like to re-read *The Emerald Tablet* (*p.11*) at this point, seeing what it says to you now. You can turn, too, to the Bibliography (*p.201*) and Further Information section (*p.205*) for ways to continue your journey here, in living the alchemy within you.

The Magnum Opus[5]
preparation:
the journey to the mine
(going in, going down)
the quest for *materia prima*
(earth: our matter, our stuff)
the Secret Fire
(meditation, contemplation)
the flask or athanor
(our container)

The Lesser Work:

NIGREDO
(Saturn)
descending, blackening
death of the ego
putrefaction
the first *coniunctio* of Sol and Luna
(untransformed sexual love)
the residue of ash
(the soul)

SOLUTIO
(Jupiter, the Moon)
ascending, whitening
cleansing of the soul
purification
the second *coniunctio* of Sol and Luna
(merging, dissolving, romantic love)
the white stone
(devotional, Christ)

The Greater Work:

COAGULATIO
(Venus and Mars)
levelling, yellowing
return to the ego = the Self
grounding
under Venus:
fermentatio
(descending)
illuminatio
(awakening)
nutrimentum
(feeding)
under Mars:
fixatio
(strengthening)
multiplicatio
(extending)
revificatio
(resurrecting)
preparation of the Stone
the third *coniunctio* of Sol and Luna
(mature, adult, differentiated love)

RUBEDO
(the Sun)
descending, ascending, reddening
the crown, fullness of the Stone, union
mortificatio
(the soul's wound, mortality)
birth of the *filius macrocosmi*
(universal consciousness: child, the Stone)
multiplicatio
(the horizontal)
projectio
(the vertical)
the fourth *coniunctio* and Royal Wedding
or Heavenly Marriage of Sol and Luna
Rex et regina, King and Queen
(spiritualized love, androgyny)
union
rippling, encircling
and closure:
(the *ouroboros* snake)
release from the flask
('in the world, but not of it')
commitment – service – Oneness
(the embodiment of spirit)

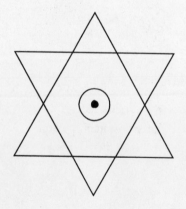

ALCHEMY & TANTRA

– BLENDING EAST AND WEST

Therefore, if we want to do something positive with our life we need a method that is at least as powerful as the confused materialistic energies we are caught up in.

LAMA THUBTEN YESHE

If a woman and a man are deeply relaxed with each other, simply meeting with each other, absorbed into each other, not in any hurry, not in any tension, many things happen, alchemical things happen – because the life-juices of both meet, the electricity of both, the bio-energy of both, meet.

BHAGWAN SHREE RAJNEESH

It didn't feel like it was generated from my own egoic sense. It was more of an etheric sense, it was outside of my body, surrounding my body. It was an energy movement. It felt like a presence, a sense in which this play was happening. This kind of archetype of love, symbol of love, was happening within this presence, this very still, rested presence.

DELL SOKOL, 'SPIRITUAL BREAKTHROUGHS IN SEX'

(RAMSEY'S ACCOUNT)

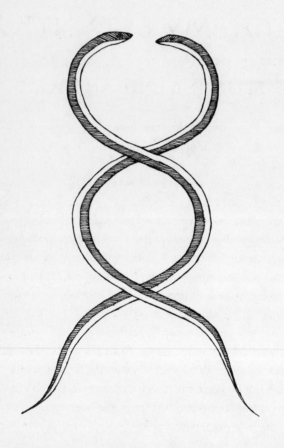

☿

ALCHEMY & TANTRA
– BLENDING EAST AND WEST

A full comparison between alchemy and tantra would be a book in itself, but because I have already mentioned tantra several times, I want to include here some of the main parallels as well as the differences. There is a real and fascinating overlap between these two areas – as between the two circles of a relationship that illuminate and strengthen each other, as distinct and individual as they also are.

Alchemy and tantra reach into very similar ground, both historically and geographically (in India), and also at a level of essence that both pre-dates and transcends place and time. There is a vital bridge between them that I think points to a greater potential wholeness between the Western and Eastern mind.

Some immediate parallels are obvious. As Philip Rawson points out,[1] tantra cannot be described as a religion as such – and neither can alchemy. Both are radical in relationship to established thinking; both have been seen as heretical and scandalous. Both validate sexuality in a unique way as an experience of transformation and as an expression of non-duality. Both emphasize process as being important. This is deepened in tantra, with its vision of a continuous present. Both use pictures (in tantra they are called *yantras*) that illustrate an understanding of what goes beyond words. In both, the red and the white denote the masculine and the feminine, although in tantra they are reversed: white is masculine and red is feminine. In both, the symbol of the snake is central, representing sexual and spiritual energy. Both are equally concerned about the body, seeing it as vital in terms of an embodied spirituality – and both avow secrecy for reasons of containment. Both processes fundamentally require a flask as an enclosed or sacred space: in both, the temple of the body is sacred. Finally, and strikingly, in both alchemy and tantra original unity is represented by a stone.

The word *tantra* means 'continuous', which suggests what is permanent within change and a quality that is without end. It goes on, just as a river keeps flowing or as rain circulates between evaporating and falling. In tantra, this is natural and supernatural at the same time.[2] The one reveals the reality of the other, in consciousness and through the body.

At the heart of tantra is a belief that our essential nature is clear and pure, and is a bliss that underlies everything. This is the gold that leads to enlightenment – and, as in alchemy, to wholeness or non-duality. Like alchemy, too, tantra asserts this as a matter of experience rather than dogma. It is not an intellectual or rational thing; it is far deeper, vaster and simpler. So, again like alchemy, tantra says this gold is within us – and the living of it is here and now. Yet it takes us beyond the life we know here as well.

Tantra goes straight for the *rubedo* in this sense, and its central emphasis, 'turning back towards the source' (*paravritti*), is essentially the same as what happens in *projectio*. At the same time, tantra recognizes what separates us from that here in the realm of *samsara* which is parallel to what alchemy identifies as ego: our desires, our demands, our fantasies and above all our grasping attachments. But rather than suppressing or denying these, tantra, like alchemy, sees that when we allow them, or include them, they in fact become the fuel for their own transmutation. Then they can change, they can be transformed. Anger can become compassion; pleasure, awareness; and emotional constriction a more spacious 'letting be'. Every state of mind or emotion can become, in Lama Yeshe's phrase 'a deep penetrative awareness' that also involves an ability to be flexible and mercurial.

Tantra is not a path of denial, then: it is a path of embracing. And it is here that it is radical. Pleasure is not the problem: it is our attachment (or addiction) to it that is. Everything in life can bring us to an awareness of essence; the problem is that we confuse what we think of as reality with it – whereas, tantra says, the essence is the *only* thing that is real and continuous. For 'essence' here we can also read, alchemically, *quintessence* and indeed, 'elixir' as well. Bliss in tantra means all of these. And, as Lama Yeshe adds:

> So we can see that the ordinary and enlightened functions of desire are directly opposed to one another. In tantra, the experience of the bliss that arises from desire expands the mind so that we overcome all our limitations, whereas ordinarily the pleasure that comes from contact with desirable objects narrows our attention and leads to a restrictive obsession for more and better pleasure.[3]

Like alchemy, too, tantra affirms our royal nature in all of this; in fact it actively encourages it as something vitally important. If we tend not to recognize reality, we recognize our own true self-worth even less, which can be equally damaging, locking us in the distortions of diminishment. In the following passage of Lama Yeshe's you can see the connection with both *revificatio* (in *coagulatio*) and *projectio* (in *rubedo*):

> One of the essential practices at all levels of tantra is to dissolve our ordinary conceptions of ourselves and then, from the empty space into which these concepts have disappeared, arise in the glorious light body of a deity: a manifestation of the essential clarity of our deepest being. The more we train to see ourselves as such a meditational deity, the less bound we will feel by life's ordinary disappointments and frustrations.[4]

Interestingly, the archetype evoked here is not so much a goddess as an archetype of *ourselves* as queen, or king. Tantra says 'as we think, so we are' and it goes on to affirm the actual effect on the physical body of a practice like this. This brings into play the healing power of the imagination itself and as such it is the opposite of self-pity. The purpose of seeing ourselves as royal in the tantric sense is designed to make us more spacious in such a way that our essence can function uninterruptedly – or 'continuously'. This is a useful way of looking at what it means to sustain kingship or queenship in the reality we live in. Tantra has a lot to teach us here.

The three main stages of tantra all have parallels with the alchemical process. The first, renunciation (which means 'emerging', here), has to do with expanding the mind from its limited perceptions, giving up unreal expectations, attaining a quality of detachment (the *rubedo*, again), and understanding the difference between satisfaction and fulfilment. 'I can't get no satisfaction' – no, you can't because it doesn't exist.

The second, *bodhicitta* (which means 'heart opening'), specifically has to do with opening to others and not just ourselves. This is where the soul warmth comes in and it corresponds to aspects of both *solutio* and *rubedo*, especially the phase of *multiplicatio*. In it we are opened to the wider concerns of people and the world, through service – and in it we attain an equanimity that sees, or begins to see, everyone as having equal importance, going beyond the distinction between friend and stranger, and even enemy.

In the third, we approach what tantra calls 'the correct view of reality', which is emptiness – not the nothingness of the Western mind, but a dissolving (again like *solutio*) in which we see that what appears permanent and solid is more like a dream. This view also applies to our identity. In tantric terms, our 'I-ness' is nothing like as solid as it seems. In realizing that, we gain a freedom, so that:

*Instead of feeling suffocated and oppressed by our surround-
ings – it's me against them – we will feel as if there is room for
everything in the world. There is space for everything. Within
the clear space of non-duality, everything flows freely in a constant process of coming and going, growing and dying, arising
and disappearing.*[5]

Here we can see that spirit and matter come together *through
the release of matter* (its loosening, its transparency) which at
the same time releases us into a state of greater naturalness, one
that you can experience, for instance, in a jacuzzi with its jets of
water pulsating and streaming. Interestingly, too, the colour here
is not red, but blue.[6]

The guru in tantra, who is both an outer master (or mistress)
and an inner guide, corresponds to the Master in alchemy who
passes on the Work, revealing the importance of our own inner
guidance in a new light. At the same time, the *vajra body* that
corresponds to the subtle or etheric body in alchemy is revealed
as the 'body of light', where the heart is the home of the subtle
mind – again in Lama Yeshe's phrase, 'the very subtle mind of
clear light'.

In the highest tantric practice, then, it is out of the marriage of
bliss and emptiness that the wedding – the *mahamudra* (or 'great
seal') – is realized. Like the *rubedo* itself, this is something we
can only experience in glimpses, and at turns, again and again.
But, as tantra would say, it is always there because it *is* reality,
behind all the veils of appearance.

So the body in tantra is precious because it contains all we
need to reach enlightenment – and here tantric writers speak of
the 'kundalini gold' and the 'kundalini oil'. Beyond this, tantra –
and Tibetan Buddhism – opens up to a whole technology of the
death process and conscious dying that is enshrined in the
Tibetan Book of the Dead. So, like alchemy, it is both a preparation for life and for death, where finally the difference between
the two is transcended through understanding essence. That is
oneness in tantric terms:

In the clear light space of emptiness there are no colours,
odours, sensations, and so on. All narrow dualistic puzzles
disappear and, as a result, the natural state of your mind
is allowed to radiate, to embrace the entire world of reality.[7]

So spirit finally infuses matter, revealing it for what it is. Tantra,
like alchemy too in the *rubedo*, speaks of various *siddhis* or
powers that a tantric adept reaches including astral projection.

Now in all of this I have said nothing so far about sexuality. In
Buddhist Tantra (Hindu Tantra is more lenient here), the three
stages they call 'generation' have to be entered into before we are
ready for the sexual embrace. Generation, which is described as a
fire in the navel area, corresponds exactly to the Secret Fire of
alchemy. It is energy, purification and restraint. If the West has
undervalued sexuality in alchemy, it has over-inflated it in
tantra, so it can seem that sex is all there is to it. At the same
time it does have a vital, unique and beautiful place – but it is
only a place we can understand when we see how different it is
from ordinary sexuality.

The generation stages accomplish something of the transmutation of the Lesser Work and *coagulatio* – especially in the separation experienced by Sol and Luna – so that:

All the old problems associated with desire will have been
solved; instead of being the cause of dissatisfaction, desire is
now fuelling the experience of totality.[8]

Then we are ready to make love and make it new. What is the
real difference? In one word, meditation. As Bhagwan Rajneesh
(now known as Osho) says rightly, 'Tantra means this: transformation of love into meditation.'[9]

And it is here that the *soror mystica* comes into her own as the
female *tantrika* where classically it is said that it is not the man
who penetrates the woman's body, but the woman's energy that
penetrates the man's. This offers us a further clue to understanding
the androgyny of the *rubedo* in terms of androgynous sexuality,

where in tantra the roles are complementary and at the same time reversed. Woman is again on top of man, but man at the same time underpins woman, and it is here he finds a different kind of maleness that contains him and roots him in his sex as himself.

The whole aim of tantric sexuality is towards continuity rather than conclusion, energy and bliss rather than a quick orgasm. Bliss is revealed as the heightened energy of love-making, and as the essence of what love-making is. It is a wedding and a blending any couple can share, and it evokes an energy, a wellness and a healing that can echo silently on for days.

In terms of alchemy, tantric sexuality is an *opus contra naturam* from the start, because it reverses the ordinary current or voltage of sex. Like alchemy, the heat needs to be gentle or the flask will crack (the man will come). Relaxation is the key here. As Rajneesh also says:

> And when you are fighting you are always outside. If you are fighting sex, you are always outside. If you surrender to sex you reach the very inner core of it, you are an insider. And if you surrender many things become known.[10]

So it is a beginning that stays in the beginning, then, where touch is slowed to the actual pace of feeling and contact, and the movement of two bodies together isn't trying to get anywhere other than *here*, in the present and 'in the presence of' where time becomes eternity. This is what tantra calls 'the valley', which is the deep place of the body as opposed to the 'peak' of mental, sexual excitation and being in one's head. In tantra then we go *down* before we ascend ... and in ascending we reach a stillness within the moving together that opens each of us to each other like a door – and through that door is space, ever-expanding space that is also inside each of our cells. So bliss touches emptiness, and in the breathing we share, a true rhythm comes into being where the love-making happens as if by itself – and then it's all turned around: *love is making us*, rather than we who are trying to make love; and it is a love that opens out everywhere, radiating peace, warmth and clarity. It is no longer confined to our immediate surroundings either: it becomes our contact with life itself. More reliable than any external chemical, it is far more quietly powerful, too.

Within it, also, we can reach what tantric practitioners have described as 'making the circle', which is another way of understanding what it means to marry ourselves – and which the *ouroboros* is an uncannily exact image for. Tantric love is a love without binding – it frees us into the circle of ourselves and into a circle we can make with anything: a lake, the landscape, the rising moon. So in this way it expands again, it takes us beyond our apparent limitations and beyond where we have tended to see sex – down the wrong end of a telescope.

Tantra's gift to alchemy is to detail the higher reaches of its sexuality. Seeing *projectio* as *paravritti* embodies it and brings it within our reach. At the same time, alchemy's gift to tantra is to remind it of its passion, its personal touch and presence. After all we are not just doors to each other: we are human beings, and soul-beings together.

There are differences too, of course. No two structures are the same. Tantra is described as quicker (as 'a lightning vehicle') where alchemy is slower, although tantric sexuality in one sense contradicts this. Tantra is perhaps more transcendent, more detached; alchemy more immanent and inclusive of our individual psyches and imaginations. Alchemy is richer here. And tantra tends to dissolve our identity at exactly the point where alchemy coagulates it (in the stone).

In the West, our strength is in our individuality – but it can also be our weakness, our pride and isolation too; and the more one looks at alchemy and tantra together, the more complementary and androgynous they become. Alchemy, like yoga,[11] is specifically more masculine in its emphasis on trial and effort; tantra is more feminine in its exalted receptivity, its yin-like genius of allowing and opening. There is so much they can realize from each other because of their differences; and then, as well as being countries apart, they are countries together – like two old lovers it is time to bring back to bed for the new world we all need to conceive and be conceived in, that is a marriage of all nations, all divisions and splits, and not only East and West.

REFERENCES

BEGINNING/INTRODUCTION
1. Duff, Kat, *The Alchemy of Illness*, Virago, 1993, p. 78.
2. Harpur, Patrick, *Mercurius: The Marriage of Heaven & Earth*, Macmillan, 1990, p. 108.
3. In *Alchemy: The secret art*, Thames & Hudson, 1973, illustrated.
4. Jarman, Derek, *Chroma*, Vintage, 1995, p. 76.
5. *Tabula Smaragdina*, Heidelberg, 1926, quoted in Titus Burckhardt's *Alchemy*, Stuart & Watkins, 1967; Element Books, 1986, pp. 196–7. Burckhardt adds his own insightful commentary.

A BRIEF HISTORY
1. See Eliade, Mircea, *The Forge and the Crucible*, p. 142, quoted in Mark Haeffner's *Dictionary of Alchemy*, Aquarian, 1991, p. 14.
2. Quoted in Thompson, C. J. S., *The Lure and Romance of Alchemy*, Harrap, 1932; Outlet/Random House, 1990, p. 17.
3. Thompson, op. cit., p. 78.
4. See Sherwood-Taylor, F., *The Alchemists*, Heinemann, 1962; Paladin, 1976, p. 95.

5. Chaucer referred to alchemy as 'this slyding science'.

6. Quoted in Thompson, op. cit., pp. 165–6.

7. Ibid., p. 170.

8. Quoted in Sherwood-Taylor, op. cit., p. 103.

9. Some of these form part of the account of the process given here.

10. See 'Solutio' (*pp.82–3*) for the white stone.

11. Quoted in Sherwood-Taylor, op. cit., pp. 111–12.

12. Ibid., p. 114.

13. The paintings in the *Splendor Solis* are by Lucas van Leiden, an early Dutch master.

14. See for instance *Songs of Innocence & Experience*, 1793.

15. Quoted in Haeffner, op. cit., p. 24.

16. See Descartes' *Principles of Natural Philosophy*, 1644.

17. As Lindsay Clarke notes, *A Suggestive Enquiry* was reissued by The Yogi Society in Britain and The Julien Press in the USA.

18. See Thompson, op. cit., p. 228.

19. See Further Information (*p.205*).

20. Quoted in Gilchrist, Cherry, *The Elements of Alchemy*, Element, 1991, pp. 119–20.

21. Ibid., p. 121.

22. *Psychology and Alchemy*, Routledge, 1953; 1993, p. 242.

23. Ibid., p. 245.

24. Ibid., p. 270.

25. For instance in Spagyrics: see *Caduceus*, issue 19, 'Alchemy and Transformation', December 1992.

26. For instance with Liz Greene, astrologer and Jungian analyst – and see Further Information (*p.205*).

27. See Johnson, Kenneth Raynor, *The Fulcanelli Phenomenon*, (Jersey, 1980), quoted by Patrick Harpur in *Mercurius*, Macmillan, 1990, p. 316. Fulcanelli, whose actual identity remains unknown, published two texts in the 1920s and was in Spain in a castle in the 1950s. He was apparently a real alchemist.

28. Quoted in Gilchrist, op. cit., p. 124.

PREPARATION

1. See Burckhardt, Titus, *Alchemy*, Stuart & Watkins, 1967;
   Element Books, 1986, p. 103.
2. Quoted in Jung, C. G., *Psychology and Alchemy*,
   Routledge, 1953; 1993; p. 320.
3. See Klossowski de Rola, Stanislaus, *Alchemy: The secret
   art*, Thames & Hudson, 1973, and for the other two phrases.
4. Quoted in Thompson, C. J. S., *The Lure and Romance of
   Alchemy*, Harrap, 1932; Outlet/Random House, 1990,
   p. 109.
5. Jung, op. cit., p. 270.

NIGREDO

1. *Caput mortuum* also refers literally to the residue left at
   the bottom of the flask – for instance the black residue of
   calcined lead. Hence the image.
2. Quoted in Fabricius, Johannes, *Alchemy: the mediaeval
   alchemists and their royal art*, Rosenkilde and Bagger,
   Copenhagen, 1976; The Aquarian Press, Wellingborough,
   UK, 1989.
3. *Musaeum hermiticum reformatum et amplificatum*,
   Frankfurt, 1678.
4. Quoted in Burckhardt, Titus, *Alchemy*, Stuart & Watkins,
   1967; Element Books, 1986, pp. 133–4 (including
   Burckhardt's comments).
5. Jung, C. G., *Psychology and Alchemy*, Routledge, 1953;
   1993, pp. 336–7.
6. The 'Saturn Return' takes place every 28 years. So next
   at age 56.
7. Fabricius, op. cit.
8. Franz, Marie-Louise von, *Alchemy: An introduction to the
   symbolism and the psychology*, Inner City Books, Toronto,
   1980, p. 147.
9. See also his 'Nigredo' in *Earth Ascending: An anthology of
   new and living poetry*, ed. Jay Ramsay, Stride Publications,
   UK, 1996.

SOLUTIO

1. Quoted in Klossowski de Rola, Stanislaus, *Alchemy: The Secret Art*, Thames & Hudson, 1973, p. 11.
2. Ibid.
3. See 'The Lapis-Christ Parallel' in Jung, C. G., *Psychology and Alchemy*, Routledge, 1953; 1993, p. 345 *et seq.*
4. Klossowski de Rola, op. cit., p. 12.
5. Quoted in Fabricius, Johannes, *Alchemy: The mediaeval alchemists and their royal art*, The Aquarian Press, 1989, p. 127.
6. Ibid., p. 130.
7. From *A Blue Fire*, ed. Thomas Moore, Routledge, 1990, p. 125.
8. Again I am indebted to Barbara Somers for her insightfulness here.
9. Franz, Marie-Louise von, *Alchemy*, Inner City Books, 1980, p. 260.
10. See Further Information, *p. 205*.
11. See also Hillman, 'On Soul and Spirit', *A Blue Fire*, op. cit., p. 124.
12. See Bly, Robert, *Iron John*, Element Books, 1991.

COAGULATIO

1. By Barbara Somers.
2. From Sendivogius, Michael, *Concerning Sulphur*, The Alchemical Press, 1991, p. 11. Sendivogius, around 1605, claimed the work of Scottish alchemist Alexander Sethon as his own, using the remains of Sethon's red tincture to establish his own reputation in Europe – for as long as it lasted. For the full story see Thompson, C. J. S., *The Lure and Romance of Alchemy*, Harrap, 1932; Outlet/Random House, 1990, pp. 188–92.
3. Quoted in Burckhardt, Titus, *Alchemy*, Stuart & Watkins, 1967; Element Books, 1986, p. 189.

4. Quoted in Fabricius, Johannes, *Alchemy: The mediaeval alchemists and their royal art*, The Aquarian Press, 1989, p. 141.
5. Quoted ibid., p. 143.
6. Ibid., p. 144.
7. Ibid., p. 146.
8. Ibid.
9. Burckhardt, op. cit., p. 190.
10. See Vermeer's painting *Woman weighing Gold* (1660–5).
11. Quoted in Fabricius, op. cit., p. 152.
12. Burckhardt, op. cit., p. 190.
13. Quoted in Fabricius, op. cit., p. 156.
14. Quoted ibid., p. 169.
15. Including Ruth White and her discarnate guide Gildas.
16. Franz, Marie-Louise von, *Alchemy*, Inner City Books, 1980, pp. 258–9.
17. Heaney, Seamus, 'The Earth House' in *Seeing Things*, Faber and Faber Ltd.
18. See *With my Heart in my Mouth*, ed. Paul Matthews, Rudolf Steiner Press, 1994, and also his *Sing Me the Creation*, Hawthorn Press, Stroud, 1995.
19. In Moore, Thomas, *Care of the Soul*, Piatkus, 1992, p. 262.
20. Ibid., p. 263.
21. In Caduceus, issue 19, 'Alchemy and Transformation', December 1992, p. 12.
22. In the seventeenth century.
23. Duff, Kat, *The Alchemy of Illness*, Virago, 1993, p. 90.
24. Fox, Matthew, *The Coming of the Cosmic Christ*, Harper & Row, 1988.
25. Jung spoke of 'the collective unconscious'. It is time, I think, to speak of 'the collective Self' in terms of what is *super*conscious.

1. From *The Collected Poems of W. B. Yeats*, Macmillan, Papermac reprint, 1985.

2. From 'Into the heart – a matrix poem' by Jay Ramsay, which forms part of *Heart of Earth*, bk. 6 of *The Great Return*, bks 1–5, The Diamond Press, 1988.

3. John Pordage, quoted in Fabricius, Johannes, *Alchemy: The mediaeval alchemists and their royal art*, The Aquarian Press, 1989, p. 173.

4. Ibid.

5. Quoted ibid., p. 174.

6. Gerard Dorn, quoted ibid., p. 177.

7. Quoted ibid., p. 178.

8. Quoted ibid., p. 175 and p. 179.

9. Ibid., p. 182.

10. Quoted from Jung's *Mysterium Coniunctionis*, ibid., pp. 182–3.

11. Quoted ibid., p. 186.

12. See Burckhardt, Titus, *Alchemy*, Stuart & Watkins, 1967; Element Books, 1986, p. 156.

13. John Pordage, quoted in Fabricius, op. cit., p. 191.

14. In Daskalos, *The Esoteric Teachings* (*see Bibliography*).

15. See Clow, Barbara Hand, *The Liquid Light of Sex*, Bear & Co., 1991, p. 103.

16. See Fabricius, op. cit., p. 198.

17. The music is available on the *Orlando* CD.

18. Jung, C. G., *Memories, Dreams, Reflections*, ed. Anelia Jaffé, Flamingo, 1983, pp. 296–7.

19. See the last page of Lindsay Clarke's *The Chymical Wedding*, Picador, 1991.

20. The *Aurora consurgens*, conceivably written by Thomas Aquinas as his last work after he abandoned the *Summa theologica*. See Franz, Marie-Louise von, *Alchemy*, Inner City Books, 1980, p. 177 *et seq.*

21. *Liber platonis quartorum*, in Fabricius, op. cit., p. 208.

22. Eliot, T. S., *Four Quartets*, Faber, 1944; frequently reprinted.

23. The essence of *rubedo* is where heart and mind come together.
24. See The Sharpham Papers no. 3, 1993.
25. Jung, C. G., *Psychology and Alchemy*, Routledge, 1953; 1993, p. 293.
26. *A Matter of Heart*, 1987. See also Jonathan Stedall's two documentaries.
27. Harpur, Patrick, 'Sublimation', *Mercurius*, Macmillan, 1990, p. 360.
28. Mother Meera, *Answers*, Meeramma Publications, 1991; republished by Rider, 1991, p. 74 in the Meerama edition.
29. In a private letter to the author.
30. Singer, June, *Androgyny*, Anchor Press/Doubleday, 1976, p. 277.
31. I am grateful to Mrs Nancy Lidell for this; source unknown.

ROSA MUNDI

The reference in the third paragraph ('Do you remember how in Heaven ...') is to Dante's vision in the *Paradiso*, which was first brought to my attention by Piero Ferrucci in a lecture he gave with slides at the Psychosynthesis Education and Trust in London, in 1986.

The allusion to 'no marrying or giving in marriage' appears in St Mark 11:25 and St Luke 20:34–5. My thanks to Madeleine O'Callaghan SSL for clarifying this.

For symbolism associated with the rose, I am indebted to Joan Cooper's *Illustrated Encyclopaedia of Traditional Symbols* (Thames & Hudson, 1973). As she says, on p. 141, the blue rose is 'the unattainable, the impossible', the Rose of the Winds 'is represented as a circle enclosing the double cross, signifying the four cardinal and four intermediate directions'; and the *Rosarium* is the philosophy and inward discipline of the Work. It is this turning inward that is the key here to a greater realization and a greater emergence.

1. Greene, Liz, with Sasportas, Howard, *Dynamics of the Unconscious*, Arkana, 1988, p. 283.

2. In conversation at her home in Stroud, Gloucestershire.

3. At The English Group at Psykisk Center, August 1995.

4. Almost certainly written while Wilde was in prison (Reading Gaol).

5. Fabricius relates each *coniunctio* to a stage of the *anima* (see Fabricius, p. 206) so that *nigredo* is connected to Eve, or sexual woman; *solutio* to Luna, as romantic woman; *coagulatio* to spiritualized woman; and *rubedo* to mystical/archetypal woman at the highest level (Dante's Beatrice, Mary, Kuan Yin), where he speaks of an androgynous element coming in. I think we need to see this the other way round too in terms of four stages of the masculine or *animus*: so with *nigredo*, we would have the 'Old Adam'; with *solutio*, the prince or romantic man; with *coagulatio*, the mature, grounded man; and with *rubedo*, the king (although the king is evident in *coagulatio* also). These would correspond to what a woman is seeing or projecting, and with both Christ and Yogananda, for instance, the androgynous element is present – with Yogananda, visibly so in photographs of him.

   Seeing what kind of man or woman we are attracted to at any stage can help us identify where we are in the process and which *coniunctio* is alive for us. You may like to draw up a parallel chart here accordingly.

APPENDIX: ALCHEMY AND TANTRA
– BLENDING EAST AND WEST

1. Rawson, Philip, *Tantra: The Indian cult of ecstasy*, Thames & Hudson, 1973. And see also his *The Art of Tantra*, Thames & Hudson, 1978, which has a full length text.

2. It is interesting to compare tantra with Taoism here. See my *Tao Te Ching*, the new translation, with Kwok Man-Ho and Martin Palmer, Element Books, 1994.

3. Landaw, Jonathan, ed., *Introduction to Tantra: A vision of totality*, Wisdom Books, Boston, 1987, p. 37.

4. Ibid., p. 42.

5. Ibid., p. 89.

6. Symbolizing non-duality.

7. Ibid., p. 133.

8. Ibid., p. 146.

9. Bhagwan, Rajneesh, *Tantra, Spirituality & Sex*, Rajneesh Foundation International, 1983.

10. Ibid., p. 120.

11. As Rajneesh points out, as part of his argument for tantra; and sexuality as something we *feel* rather than something we force. This is the difference.

SELECT BIBLIOGRAPHY

ESSENTIAL READING

Burckhardt, Titus, *Alchemy*, Stuart & Watkins, 1967; Element
  Books, 1986

Fabricius, Johannes, *Alchemy: the mediaeval alchemists and
  their royal art*, Rosenkilde and Bagger, Copenhagen, 1976;
  The Aquarian Press, 1989

Franz, Marie-Louise von, *Alchemy*, Inner City Books, Toronto,
  1980

Haeffner, Mark, *Dictionary of Alchemy*, Aquarian, 1991

Jung, C. G., *Psychology and Alchemy*, Routledge, 1953; 1993

Klossowski, de Rola, Stanislaus, *Alchemy: The secret art*,
  Thames & Hudson, 1973

HISTORY

Gilchrist, Cherry, *The Elements of Alchemy*, Element Books,
  1991

Sherwood-Taylor, F., *The Alchemists*, Paladin, 1976

Thompson, C. J. S., *The Lure and Romance of Alchemy*,
  Random House reprint, 1990

SECONDARY

Anderton, William, *Inner Alchemy*, Soluna Publications, 1981

Caron, M. and Hutin, S., *The Alchemists*, Evergreen, 1961

Courdet, A., *Alchemy: The Philosopher's Stone*, Wildwood House, 1980

Greene, Liz and Sasportas, Howard, *Dynamics of the Unconscious*, Arkana, 1989

Holmyard, E. J., *Alchemy*, Penguin, 1957

Matthews, Caitlín and John, *The Western Way*, vol. 2, The Hermetic Tradition, Arkana, 1986

Pritchard, Alan, *Alchemy*, Routledge & Kegan Paul, 1980

Raphael, A., *The Philosopher's Stone*, Routledge, 1965

Read, John, *Through Alchemy to Chemistry*, G. Bell, 1957

Reyner, J. H., *The Diary of a Modern Alchemist*, Neville Spearman, 1974

Sadoul, Jacques, *Alchemists and Gold*, Neville Spearman, 1972

Sapere, Aude, *The Science of Alchemy*, Neptune Press, 1979

Silberer, Herbert, *Hidden Symbolism of Alchemy and the Occult Arts*, Dover, 1971

Wilson, Frank Avray, *Alchemy as a Way of Life*, C. W. Daniel, 1976

RELATED

Barbault, Armand, *Gold of a Thousand Mornings*, Neville Spearman, 1975

Bennell, M. and Wyatt, I., *The Chymical Wedding of Christian Rosencreutz*, Temple Lodge Press, 1989

Cockren, Archibald, *Alchemy Discovered and Restored*, Health Research, California, 1963

Cooper, Joan, *Chinese Alchemy*, Aquarian, 1984

Daskalos, *The Esoteric Teachings*, 1990, available from PO Box 8347, Nicosia, Cyprus

Gilbert, R. A., *The Golden Dawn: Twilight of the magicians*, Aquarian, 1983

Read, John, *The Alchemist in Life, Literature and Art*, T. Nelson, 1947

Sendivogius, Michael, *Concerning Sulphur*, The Alchemical
    Press, 1991
Sutherland, C. H. V., *Gold*, Thames & Hudson, 1959
Waite, A. E., *The Hermetic Museum, restored and enlarged*,
    Watkins, 1953

IN THE WIDER SPHERE
Bly, Robert, *A Little Book on the Human Shadow*,
    HarperCollins, 1988
Clarke, Lindsay, *The Chymical Wedding: A romance*,
    Cape/Picador, 1989
—, *Alice's Masque*, Jonathan Cape, 1994
Coelho, Paulo, *The Alchemist: A fable about following your
    dreams*, HarperSanFrancisco, 1993
Duff, Kat, *The Alchemy of Illness*, Virago, 1993
Ferrucci, Piero, *What We May Be: The visions and techniques
    of Psychosynthesis*, Turnstone Press, 1982
Harpur, Patrick, *Mercurius, or the Marriage of Heaven
    and Earth*, Macmillan, 1990
Jarman, Derek, *Chroma: A book of colour*, Vintage, 1995
Miller, Richard and Iona, *The Modern Alchemist*, Phanes Press,
    USA, 1994
Moore, Thomas, ed., *A Blue Fire: The essential James Hillman*,
    Routledge, 1990
Moore, Thomas, *Care of the Soul*, Piatkus, 1992
—, *Soul Mates*, Element, 1994
Redgrove, Peter, *The Black Goddess and the Sixth Sense*,
    Bloomsbury, 1989
Redgrove, Peter and Shuttle, Penelope, *Alchemy for Women*,
    Rider, 1995
Singer, June, *Androgyny*, Anchor/Doubleday, 1976
Whitmore, Diana, *Psychosynthesis in Education*, Turnstone
    Press, 1986

POETRY

Bletsoe, Elisabeth, *The Regardians: A book of angels*, Odyssey, 1993

Cluysenaar, Anne, *New & Selected Poems*, Carcanet, 1996

Jope, Norman, *The Wedding Guest*, Stride Publications, 1996

Moat, John, *Skeleton Key*, Phoenix Press, 1981. See *Transformation*, below.

—, *Firewater & The Miraculous Mandarin*, Enitharmon, 1990

Ramsay, Jay, ed., *Transformation: The poetry of spiritual consciousness*, Rivelin Grapheme, 1988

—, *Earth Ascending: An anthology of new & living poetry*, Stride Publications, 1996

Redgrove, Peter, *The Moon Disposes: Selected poems*, Secker & Warburg, 1988

LOVE AND SEXUALITY

Evola, Julius, *The Metaphysics of Sex*, Inner Traditions, 1983

Feuerstein, George, ed., *Enlightened Sexuality*, The Crossing Press, 1989

Keen, Sam, *The Passionate Life: Stages of loving*, Harper & Row, 1983

Lidell, Lucy, *The Sensual Body*, Unwin Hyman, 1987

Lilar, Suzanne, *Aspects of Love in Western Society*, Panther, 1967

Rajneesh, Bhagwan Shree, *Tantra, Spirituality & Sex*, Rajneesh Foundation, 1983

Rawson, Philip, *The Art of Tantra*, Thames & Hudson, 1978

Singer, June, *Androgyny*, Anchor/Doubleday, 1976

Stevens, J., *Lust for Enlightenment*, Shambhala, 1990

Yeshe, Lama, *Introduction to Tantra*, Wisdom Books, 1987

FURTHER INFORMATION

ORIGINAL TEXTS

The original alchemical texts that I know of that are in print include the following:

Turba philosophorum, ed. J. F. Ruska, Berlin, 1931
Theatrum Chemicum Britannicum, ed. Elias Ashmole, 1652
Aurora Consurgens, ed. Marie Louise von Franz, London, 1966
Hermetic Museum, ed. A. E. Waite, 1893; 2 vols
Bibliotheca chemica curiosa, ed. James Young, London, 1954

For quotations from the *Rosarium philosophorum*, I am indebted to Johannes Fabricius, who was drawing on Jung's work on the *Artis auriferae quam chemiam vocant* of 1572 and 1593, published in Germany in 1610.

The texts cited above are all major, including the two classic anthologies edited by Ashmole and A. E. Waite. Various writers on alchemy, including Titus Burckhardt and F. Sherwood-Taylor, have called for reprints of these and we are certainly ripe for another anthology here. The best contemporary example of this is *The Magnum Opus Hermetic Sourceworks*, ed. Adam McLean, published by David Fidelier at Phanes Press, PO Box 6114, Grand

Rapids, Michigan 49516, USA. The series includes Maier's *Atalanta fugiens*, and the *Splendor solis*, among others. The texts are just as revelatory in their own way as the now famous Gnostic Gospels.

If you want to see or consult texts like these, the place to go is the British Museum. Another major collection is housed in the University Library in Copenhagen, as Fabricius mentions, if you happen to be in Denmark.

CURRENT JOURNALS

One current alchemical journal in the UK is *The Hermetic Journal*, ed. Adam Maclean in Edinburgh. F. Sherwood-Taylor was the editor of another, *Ambix*, while he was alive. *Sphinx*, which is a journal of archetypal psychology, ed. Noel Cobb, often includes alchemical themes, as well as James Hillman's essays which are always (like Hillman himself) fresh, challenging and inspiring.

COURSES AND THERAPY

In the USA there is a postal course on alchemy which is available from Bill van Doren, PO Box 11218, Boulder, Colorado 80301.

On the Internet, there is the Alchemy Virtual Library and the Alchemy Forum archive, both of which contain a wealth of information, including some original texts you can access (like the *Book of Lambspring*).

For details of my workshops that include alchemy, poetry, the *I Ching* and self-development, as well as my one-to-one sessions in London and Gloucestershire, please write with a stamped addressed envelope to the Chrysalis Office, 226 London Road, Cheltenham, Glos. GL52 6HW. (Tel. 01242–528363).

If specific things have come up for you as a result of working with this book, you can contact me personally for a session (please mark your envelope 'one-to-one sessions'). You may already be seeing a therapist or you may choose to find one in your area who is sympathetic to the imagination and the spirit. We can't always work through all these things alone: our need for each other here is part of our interconnectedness that alchemy testifies to, and a good therapeutic relationship can provide an invaluable flask or container as well as being a mirror to our emerging selves, bringing us to our own truth and guidance so we can live more of who we are.

If your need is for a stronger contact with the physical body, in learning to live more *in* your body, bodywork like massage therapy may be as useful, particularly in giving our bodies time to feel which is also where we are *with soul*. There are many related disciplines here (including Reiki and Shiatsu as well as Rosen therapy), as well as the use of flower remedies and homoeopathy which are more overtly alchemical in their effect.

TANTRA
Tantra workshops are run in the UK based on the work of Margo Anand Naslednikov. You can contact SkyDancing UK (Monica Entmayr and John Hawken) at 47 Maple Road, Horfield, Bristol BS7 8RE (0117–9830958) for information. There is also a video called *Sacred Sex: A higher level of sexual fulfilment*, directed by Cynthia Connop and produced by VCI Distribution (1992). Alan Lowen's work through Art of Being is also related here (information tel. 01795–53472). This is work which is having a growing impact.

The important thing overall is to find what you need, and act on it.

J.R.

INDEX

ILLUSTRATIONS

The figure illustrations by Helen Elwes are drawn from sixteenth and seventeenth century originals reproduced in the following books:

Fabrichius, Johannes. *Alchemy: the medieval alchemists and their royal art*, Aquarian, 1989.
von Franz, Marie Louise. *Alchemy: an introduction to the symbolism and psychology*, Inner City Books, 1982
Jung, C. G. *Psychology and Alchemy*, Routledge, 1990
Rawson, Philip. *Tantra, the Indian Cult of Ecstacy*, Thames & Hudson, 1973.
Klossowski de Rola, Stanislas. *Alchemy: the secret art*, Thames & Hudson, 1973.